JOYCE TAYLOR

a *Pocketful* of
MONKEY-NUTS

Memories of a wartime childhood on Severnside

JOYCE TAYLOR

a Pocketful of
MONKEY-NUTS

Memories of a wartime childhood on Severnside

MEREO
Cirencester

Mereo Books

1A The Wool Market Dyer Street Cirencester Gloucestershire GL7 2PR
An imprint of Memoirs Publishing www.mereobooks.com

A pocketful of monkey-nuts: 978-1-86151-244-4

First published in Great Britain in 2014
by Mereo Books, an imprint of Memoirs Publishing

The address for Memoirs Publishing Group Limited can be found at
www.memoirspublishing.com

The Memoirs Publishing Group Ltd Reg. No. 7834348

Cover design - Ray Lipscombe

The Memoirs Publishing Group supports both The Forest Stewardship Council® (FSC®) and
the PEFC® leading international forest-certification organisations. Our books carrying both the
FSC label and the PEFC® and are printed on FSC®-certified paper. FSC® is the only
forest-certification scheme supported by the leading environmental organisations including
Greenpeace. Our paper procurement policy can be found at
www.memoirspublishing.com/environment

Typeset in 12/18pt Plantin
by Wiltshire Associates Publisher Services Ltd.

Printed and bound in Great Britain by
Marston Book Services Limited, Oxfordshire

Contents

Foreword
Acknowledgements
Dedication

Foreword

As we grow older and think back to our childhood, that far-off time seems such a fleeting part of our existence. But it was a time when our senses were at their keenest as we absorbed everything around us. Certain scents, sights and sounds in later life can bring the memories flooding back; for me it is the smell of pine timber and tarred marline, the sight and sound of a steam train puffing out clouds of smoke or the taste of goat's milk.

And there was no grey area to our emotions; everything was black or white. Such as the anger at a punishment you thought unjustly deserved, or the boredom and impatience of waiting for a coming treat, or the fear of the dark and imagining long hands coming out to grab you. Or the tingling anticipation of a favourite game and, of course, the thrill and excitement of Christmas. All were felt with such intensity. Also the unbearable longing you felt for something denied to you. I yearned for black patent leather shoes which fastened with ankle straps and a little round button at the front. I never got them, but on the whole, my childhood was a happy one and I hope you enjoy reading about it.

J W Taylor

Acknowledgements

I would like to thank my daughters, Elaine, Mandy and Diane, for their interest and encouragement.

For my granddaughter, Suzanne.

BEGINNINGS

Our street looked different that morning. It was usually drab and grey with rows of red brick houses lining each side, all looking exactly alike with grey slate roofs and chimneys sending out curling wisps of smoke and wooden railings bordering the tiny front gardens. The only signs of life would be a husband setting off for work in his flat cap and hobnailed boots, or women in their floral cross-over pinnies shaking a mat or a duster and occasionally stopping to gossip with a neighbour.

But that day I stared in amazement. Red, white and blue bunting was coming out of bedroom windows on one side of the street and disappearing into those opposite. All along the street were rows and rows of it, and it flapped and snapped in the breeze. The little wooden railings looked pretty with strips of crepe paper in red, white and blue twisted around them. There were canopies over doorways and awnings over gateways, all in red, white and blue. Flags were everywhere; also shields of St George with a big red cross on a white background and huge lettering saying 'GV1R'. I wondered who could have done all this while I slept.

I was ushered along the street to where my aunts, uncles and cousins were gathered. Everyone was smiling and dressed in their best clothes, quite different to their weekday appearance. They were wearing different hats, gold crowns and peaked caps, and sporting red, white and blue bosses in their buttonholes. They stood in a group urging me to join them, but I was apprehensive. What was happening in my safe, secure, little world? I didn't understand it at all.

And there was a strange man standing in Auntie Lil's garden. Whatever was he doing there? He had a strap around his neck which had a black box dangling from it. I looked at him and he looked at me and to my horror he caught hold of the black box and pointed it straight at me. I was about to be shot!

The panic that had been slowly building up boiled over and I screamed loudly, turned on my heel and ran yelling back along the street to be safely gathered up into the arms of my mother.

The date of this first memory was 12th May 1937; the celebration was for the coronation of King George VI, and I was just three years old. Now, whenever I look at the black and white photograph and see the smiling group celebrating the Coronation, I wish I was on it along with my brother, cousins, aunts and uncles. In the background is Auntie Lil's house, all gaily festooned, and the party are stood underneath a decorated arbour. Uncle Bert is on the left in the back row line-up. He must have been at the end of the line when the fancy hats were handed out, because he is wearing a schoolboy's cap perched jauntily on the side of his head. Auntie Lil is next to him and she sports a red, white and blue peaked cap and wears a rosette in her jacket. Her dress is soft fabric, because she has a floppy bow at her neck. In the centre is my grandfather; I didn't know him very well as he died when I was small. Auntie Dor and Uncle Dave complete the back row, and Auntie Dor's dress has a lovely white lacy collar. The men are in shirts and waistcoats and have rolled up their sleeves; it must have been a fine May day. But grandfather is well wrapped up and is wearing a pullover and coat on top of his waistcoat. They all look very happy, as if they are having a good time.,

In the front row, sitting on the pavement, are the children; my brother Henry and my cousins Anita and Vernon. Henry's hat is a smart crown with a silver badge on the front, while Anita and Vernon have peaked caps. Nipper, the black and white terrier, has wandered into the picture to be captured for posterity. I wonder how I would have looked. What would I be dressed in and what kind of hat would I have had?

My parents never owned a camera, so I have no photograph of myself until I was in my first year at school. I was about four then and too shy to hold my head up and smile for the camera; my head is on the side and my hair has escaped from its ribbon and it is hanging over my face. My shoulders are hunched and my eyes are partly closed as I screw them up against the sun. Photos were taken outside then, and I hated it.. In due course I took home this masterpiece and on looking at it the family hooted with laughter and made fun at my expense.

'She's got one eye shut,' mocked my brother.

'Well, I'd better draw it in then,' said Dad, and he reached up to the mantelpiece and dug around in a vase for a stub of pencil. He dabbed it on his tongue a few times and stabbed at the photo, leaving a black dot for my eye.

'Ha ha, she looks cross-eyed now,' laughed Henry.

'Well' said Dad, 'I'd better draw in the other one.' And he did.

On these special occasions of jubilees, coronations and VE Day our parties were always held in the street. Trestle tables were set up along the length of it and we sat down to a party tea, the food being donated by everyone in the street. Mam's speciality was jam tarts, always with a blob of mock cream on top, which went down very well. We enjoyed the different food provided from other mothers while they served us all with tea to drink from huge enamel jugs. Later in the evening someone would haul Mrs Griffey's piano out of her front room into her garden and she played popular tunes of the day. We sang and danced and did the Hokey Cokey, or someone started the Conga and everyone else joined on the end until we moved snake-like up and down the street long after darkness fell.

The street was part of a group of houses built at Sharpness Docks, on the east bank of the Severn estuary in Gloucestershire, for the workers and their families. There were about thirty houses in all on that part of the dock, which consisted of Bridge Road and

Dinmore Road. The rows of terraced houses were in the shape of a T. Bridge Road formed the top of the T and looked out on to the comings and goings of the dock. Halfway along Bridge Road was a gap and Dinmore Road formed the down stroke of the T. Some houses were larger than others, the ones on the ends of the rows, and had bigger gardens; these were reserved for more important workers such as the dock policemen.

The same people lived in these houses all the time I was growing up. Nothing seemed to change. There were certain ones who were more important than others, such as Charlie Beard who drove the ambulance. He was always called on to administer first aid if someone had had an accident such as a cut or a fall. 'Get Charlie to have a look at it,' would be the cry. And Mrs Hinks was the only one with a car and telephone. Many was the time Mam dashed over the street to get her to phone for the doctor. Mam always left a sixpence on the red plush tablecloth in payment. Mrs Hinks walked with a limp and had one finger missing on one hand which I always viewed with childish curiosity. She was always ready to help anyone in need.

I lived at Number 11 Bridge Road. It was situated on the corner of the gap so we had the best of both worlds. The front of the house was in Bridge Road and the side was in Dinmore Road, so we had open views of the dock and the closeness of the street.

The living room was the hub of the house and always seemed to have a coal fire burning in the grate. As well as for warmth, it was used to cook our food to save the gas. Mam always boiled the potatoes on it for our dinner and sometimes a big old black saucepan full of potato peelings would be boiling away to feed the pig. The pans were all black from the soot and if one boiled over there was much hissing and spitting as the water hit the hot coals and sent up little clouds of ash.

The kettle was always singing on the hob ready for a pot of tea and we always made our toast on it with a long-handled toasting fork, but we toasted ourselves as well as the bread. If the toasting fork was in use, Dad grabbed the bone-handled carving knife and jabbed it into a slice of bread and held it against the coals, where it sometimes collapsed and folded over, causing much muttering and complaining from Dad. At bedtime Mam warmed a saucepan of milk to be poured on to cubes of bread and sprinkled with sugar for my supper. I hugged the warm dish close and enjoyed it before going up to bed.

Mam also used the fire to heat up her flat irons. She would iron with one while the other was getting hot, then swap them over. She never used an ironing board but ironed on the scrubbed deal table, well-padded with sheets. She thought proper ironing boards were too wobbly. The freshly-ironed clothes would be neatly folded and hung to air on twine which had been spread criss-cross about the ceiling. They stayed up there for weeks sometimes - we just pulled off what we needed and Mam adding to them each week. In desperation Dad would exclaim, 'Can't we have them decorations down yet, Win?'

Above the fireplace was a wide mantelpiece, too high for me to reach, and full of all manner of things; a tin of spills for Dad to light his cigarettes with from the fire, a comb, hair clips, a box of matches, cycle clips, armbands and always at each end vases stuffed with oddments; bits of string, ends of pencils, hair curlers and odd tickets.

There were fireplaces in all the rooms, including the bedrooms, but it was rare to see a fire anywhere else in the house. Perhaps Mam would light one in the front room at Christmas as a treat or in a bedroom if anyone was ill, but it was around the living room fire that we all gathered.

In front of the fire was a rag rug. Handmade by the family to while away the winter evening, it had been made by pulling strips of cloth through hessian. The strips were about four inches long and an inch wide. A special tool was pushed through the backing, then the end of a strip was held and it was tugged through. Everyone had a rag bag then; there were no charity shops needing unwanted clothes. Anyway, money for new clothes was so short that clothes were either grown out of or worn till they fell to pieces. The materials in the bag were still of use; best bits of tablecloths became tea towels, sheets were torn up as dusters and old towels made good flannels and floor cloths

So out of this bag came stuff for our mat-making. Old wool coats, trousers and skirts were useful. The border of the mat was usually dark, navy or brown and the centre was a hotchpotch of colours, depending on the fabric available. A new rug was started with enthusiasm, but it was an arduous business and became a bit of a chore with people complaining of sore fingers with so much tugging. But eventually it was finished and greatly admired as it took pride of place in front of the fire.

The rest of the floor was covered with linoleum. Dad had his own armchair; very simple with wooden arms and cushions. It was always Dad's chair and usually had a bottle of cider on the floor alongside of it. There was a similar chair the other side of the fire and a sideboard in the room. But it was around the plain scrubbed table that we sat for our meals and at other times too. We enjoyed a game of whist in the evenings. I always felt excitement as Dad reached up into the cupboard for the pack of cards. We paired off in twos and Dad dealt out the cards.

'Right then, what's trumps? You go first, our Joyce.'

I put down the first card. 'Go on Mam, your turn.'

'Damn my buttons!' exclaimed Dad, 'What did you do that for? You've thrown away a good card there.'

'Right then, beat that,' shouted Henry as he slapped his card on the table. 'That game's mine.'

The table was also used for working on. Henry built his Meccano up on it and I did colouring or homework.

The wireless was a great favourite in the evenings. On Sunday nights we listened to the music from Grand Hotel. Albert Sandler played the violin with the Palm Court Orchestra. Dad enjoyed ITMA (It's That Man Again) with Tommy Handley and Mam's favourite was Twenty Questions, when a panel of four well-known people had to guess a subject and were allowed only twenty questions to do it. All these programmes were on the Light Programme as well as the popular music of the day. There was also the Home Service for more serious talk, including the news. And the Third Programme was for classical music. These were the only programmes on radio then, and of course there was no television.

The kitchen was tiny with rough, red flagstones on the floor which had to be scrubbed regularly. There was a gas stove and a small table for the preparation of food, as well as a few shelves for pots and pans. That was all there was room for. There was a sink which was brown earthenware, smooth and rough in patches, but the one thing I remember about it was the huge cavernous hole in one corner where all manner of things disappeared, mainly teaspoons, and Mam was adept at going outside and putting her hand down the drain and retrieving them.

We had no bathroom, so we washed ourselves at the kitchen sink. During the war we had some lodgers. The Carriers were from Doncaster and Mr Carrier was a soldier stationed at Sharpness. If they could find anyone to put them up they were allowed to bring their wives for a short stay. Mrs Carrier always seemed posh to me; a nice-looking woman with light brown curly hair. One day she was washing herself in the kitchen when she suddenly set up such a wailing. 'Mrs Bennett, my teeth, my teeth they've gone down the plughole!' She was beside herself with grief.

'Oh, don't you worry, we'll soon have them back' said Mam. Nothing worried her. She went outside and plunged her hand into the greasy water and felt around for a bit and soon held the dentures aloft, much to the relief of their owner.

We had a larder; big enough to go into and shut the door. It was dark inside as it just had a small area covered with zinc gauze in one wall to let in air and keep out flies. I crept in from time to time to see what could be found. My little hand dug into bags of raisins, or better still if Mam had opened a tin of condensed milk to go on our Sunday rhubarb tart. I spooned it out straight into my mouth. Lovely! Needless to say some tasty morsels were put high up on the top shelf where greedy little people couldn't reach.

The water had to be fetched from the pump which was just outside our back gate. Always very cold and pure, it was carried in buckets and stood in the kitchen ready for use. Although we had no water laid on in the kitchen, we always had a flush lavatory. The door to it would have been outside if we hadn't had the lean-to over the kitchen, so this stopped prying eyes on our meanderings to and fro. This was just as well, because if Mam had dosed me with liquorice powder or liquid paraffin, as was the habit in those days, I had to get out of bed and make a quick trip to the lavvy in the darkness of the night. For our toilet paper, if Mam had time she cut up neat little squares of newspaper and threaded them with string through one corner then hung them on a nail, but more often than not the whole Daily Herald was just slung in on to the floor.

On bath nights, once a week, the old tin bath was unhooked from its nail on the wall out the back and carried into the kitchen, or in front of the living room fire if it was cold, and then filled laboriously with buckets of hot water that had been heated in the boiler. An electric boiler was modern then. Before that I know they had a copper with a fire underneath, but my memory doesn't stretch back that far. The same water was used by all the family, just warmed up a bit each time, so you were lucky if you were the first one in. The side of the bath nearest to the fire got very hot and you had to be careful not to touch it. But it was luxury to step out and be cocooned in towels that had been warmed by the fire.

Monday was always washday and Mam worked hard that day. Dad filled the electric boiler ready and switched it on, having carried buckets of water from the pump. Mam boiled all the whites; sheets, pillow cases and towels. She thought they weren't clean without a good boil; the house was full of the smell of soap and boiling clothes. Several small baths were put in place and the clothes sorted into piles: whites, coloureds and darker, dirtier items such as working trousers or overalls.

The coloured things were put to soak in soapy water. The powders weren't so good as today; no biological, just Persil or Rinso. The dirty overalls had to be scrubbed by hand, and the handkerchiefs too, which wasn't very pleasant when someone had a bad cold. These were the days before paper tissues.

After several rinses in clean changes of water, with a squeeze of a blue bag in the final rinse, which was supposed to make the whites look whiter, she put the lot through a wringer, puffing and panting as she turned the handle. Then it was hung out to dry on the line and flapped in the breeze. Any hot soapy water left over was used to scrub down the yard.

Mam broke off at dinner time. Our dinner that day was always slices of cold meat from Sunday's joint and bubble and squeak, a mixture of left over vegetables – cabbage or sprouts chopped with potato, and fried in the pan till brown and crispy, then turned over and cooked on the other side. After we had eaten Mam went back to the washtub, mainly finishing off, but washing was hard and tiring work then. She always used Glymiel Jelly to rub on her poor chapped hands; rubber gloves were not available, but she couldn't afford them anyway.

The front room was the best room and hardly used. The door to it opened straight in from the street and I only remember it being used to admit the doctor when he called or to let me out as a young bride. It had to be primed in readiness; the thick, dark brown velvet curtain that hung over it had to be yanked back on its pole and as it was forced open paint cracked and hinges groaned at the sudden onslaught. A few pushes and pulls, which let in an abnormal amount of light and fresh air, and it was ready for use.

This room came into its own at Christmas when, for a treat, a coal fire burned in the pretty Victorian grate. It gave the room a cosy glow and different smells; dampness drying out and the baking of the cover of the three-piece suite when it stayed too close to the fire. The brown Rexine covering, a sort of imitation leather, became hard and crispy and, with the help of little fingers, disgorged its sawdust filling. 'Push that chair back from the fire!' yelled Mam. When the highly-polished oak table with its barley sugar legs had a big glass bowl of oranges on the top, I knew Christmas had arrived.

THE DOCK

The street where I lived was in Sharpness, a small inland port on the River Severn about halfway between Gloucester and Bristol. There had been a dock at Sharpness since 1818. 'Ness' means promontory, and where the first dock was situated there is a sharp point of land jutting out into the Severn. It was always called The Point. Westwards across the Severn is Lydney and the Forest of Dean

With its links to Gloucester and the Midlands, Sharpness has always been looked upon as a favourable trade route and by the late 1860s trade was being turned away because the dock was too small. Permission had to be granted through Parliament for a new dock and then money was raised through loans and shares to buy farmland, much to the dislike of the wealthy landowners, and the dock that I knew was carved out of daisy-studded meadows. When the heavy clay soil was excavated a submerged forest was found, thought to have begun when the climate warmed after the Glacial Period, with trees of oak, beech and hazel. There were also remains of animals; cattle, deer and the tusk of a wild boar.

The new dock covered about twenty acres. At its entrance from the Severn there were two piers, a tidal basin, locks and a dry dock for repairs. At the other end there were two road bridges, the High and the Low bridge and an area of water known as the Cut which ran into the Berkeley and Gloucester Canal. The canal, completed in 1827, was a safer route to Gloucester, as beforehand ships used to sail on up the Severn with its dangerous shifting sandbanks.

When I was growing up in the 30s and 40s the dock was always very busy and full of ships carrying cargoes from all over the world. Timber, mostly spruce and pine, came from the Baltic and Canada, but also teak from Burma. Grain came from Russia, Australia, Canada and America, cotton seed from India, ground nuts from West Africa and demerara sugar from Barbados.

The scene of timber sheds, towering grain silos, dusty red brick warehouses, huge cargo ships and jibs of cranes piercing the sky was my world, and we looked out on it all from home. Roads were criss-crossed with railway lines which, if I wasn't careful, trapped the front wheel of my bicycle and threw me off. Engines hissed with steam and covered everything in black smuts as they shunted cargo-laden trucks about, much to the disgust of housewives on washdays, as the lines ran right alongside the houses.

Everywhere, during those busy days, was stack upon stack of

timber. My dad was a stevedore or docker as we called them. When he was deal (timber) 'tumping' he always wore a leather pad over his shoulder for protection, but many times I watched him grimace with pain as he eased off his shirt to reveal a red swollen shoulder. The pad was stiff dark brown leather, shiny with wear, and was tied with a lace under his arm. The timber, or deals as we called them, were all manhandled by dockers from ship to shore.

On ship two men lifted the deals on to a man's shoulder, where they balanced at the centre point and the ends swayed up and down. The run from ship to shore was made of heavy planks supported on trestles and as the men bounced along the planks with their load they set up an oscillation. The planks rattled as they jogged and the wood was offloaded onto the pile with a loud slap. They returned to the ship for another load along a different route of planks and trestles while another man, loaded with deals, bounced along the first route. As the timber stack got higher so did the staging, and if the men were on piecework – perhaps the ship had to sail on the next tide – they worked nonstop. The air was full of the sound of boots on wood and the crack of the deals as they reached their destination.

The timber was loaded on to lorries and taken away by road or into lighters to be towed up the canal to Morelands' match factory, or to sawmills and timber yards along the canal. But many were stored at Sharpness and when timber sheds were full the wood was stacked on any spare ground available.

The timber sheds were great places for children. They were

our world of make believe. 'See you tomorrow in the timber sheds,' was always our parting shot as we were hauled off to bed each night. The sheds were huge open-sided affairs constructed of cast iron pillars with corrugated iron roofs and concrete floors. The rough timber deal planks were uniform and neat on the outside, but inside was a myriad of lengths and thicknesses. We ran from one to another to see which was the springiest to be used as a trampoline, oblivious of the fact that the whole lot could come tumbling down on us. Spaces created between the deals were perfect for playing shops; a long plank became the counter and we made provisions with mud and moss. We played houses in all the nooks and crannies, and hide and seek or 'sardines' until darkness fell and we heard our mother's voices calling us home. Splintery and full of the scent of pine resin, it was warm and out of cold winds in winter but cool and shady in summer, and the place where we shared our innermost secrets.

Coils of rope usually lay around, and one enterprising boy was always ready to show off his skills; he grabbed a rope and shinned up the iron girder to the roof, which was very high. He eased himself, bit by bit, along a rafter with the rope until he was almost at the centre, eagerly watched by a crowd of children below, and slung the rope over where it uncoiled as it flew through the air and hit the ground with a loud slap. He secured it to the rafter with knots and made his way down. Another huge knot was tied in the end as a seat and we clambered on. Just one or two to start, but then another and another climbed on until we were all flying high through the air back and forth, perhaps six or eight of us. We could see over the rooftops and the rope creaked loudly high up in the rafters with every heart-stopping swing. Eventually our arms grew tired and the rough rope stung our tender legs and hands, so we could hold on no longer and slithered off to the floor; a laughing, screaming jumble of children.

Another childhood game was hopscotch; the grid was chalked on to the road. Only occasionally did we have to stop and wait for a car to pass. There were few cars at Sharpness. Mr Mahoney, the local chemist, had one; it was two-tone brown and black, like a big box on wheels, and he sat up on high in the driving seat. Ted Fryer from the farm had a maroon and black one; again like a box on wheels but smaller. Of course, Mr Bradley, the dock manager, had one, a smart black saloon. If anyone bought a car the buzz went round as people passed on the news. It was the same in the 50s when people bought their first television set. 'Peglar's got a television, did you see the aerial go up?'

We played with balls, sometimes juggling three or four in the air at the same time. Handstands up against the wall was another favourite. Skipping too, either with an individual rope or a long one, with a girl on each end to twirl it. We chanted rhymes as we skipped. All these games needed very little apparatus and kept us fit. The boys played marbles, conkers or bowled an old bicycle tyre along with a stick. Carts were made out of orange boxes and old pram wheels, with thick string to tow them along. Japanese knotweed grew on a bank nearby and we cut the stalks, which were hollow, and made peashooters out of them. Sometimes we clambered into punts moored in the cut, a stretch of water joining the dock with the canal just under the High Bridge, and dabbled our hands in the water. We were free, more or less, to wander anywhere. We kept a look out for the dock police and dodged them if they appeared, but they were a friendly lot and were there for our own good. One, a Mr Woolley, cut hair as a sideline and the boys said he put a basin on their head and cut off any hair that was sticking out.

Grain came into the dock in enormous vessels of 5,000 to 6,000 tons. It was a dusty cargo and with the wind in the right direction windowsills and washing became covered in a grey powder and a pungent grainy smell filled the air. When Dad worked on it he came home looking as if he had put his face into a bag of flour and blown hard; his eyebrows, lashes and hair were thick with dust.

Most of the grain was ready bagged, each bag weighing two and a quarter hundredweight, but sometimes it came in bulk and had to be weighed out by the bushel on shore before being tipped into chutes or onto conveyer belts to be stored in the warehouses. Men carried the bags on their backs and wore capes with hoods made of hessian to protect them from the dust, and each man had string tied tightly around his trouser legs just below the knee. Dad said it was to stop the rats running up their legs.

The grain was transported in barges up the canal to flour mills at Tewkesbury, Worcester and on up to Pershore, or by lorry and road to manufacturers of animal foodstuffs. When it dropped on the dockside it gave off a stench as it rotted, but some germinated in ruts of railway lines or sides of buildings and sent up green shoots which looked bright and fresh amid the greyness of the dock. Dad was allowed to bring home sweepings from the dockside to feed the chickens, and sometimes other dockers arrived with a bucket of grain in exchange for a few eggs.

Coal was another messy cargo and Dad looked like a minstrel when he came home; all I could see was the whites of his eyes and his pink mouth when he spoke, otherwise he was all black and didn't look like my father. The galvanised bath had to be brought in each day when he unloaded coal.

Of all the commodities which came into Sharpness, the ones favoured by us children were of course the ones we could eat. One was peanuts, or monkey-nuts as we called them. 'There's a monkey-nut boat in!' someone would shout, and our meanderings took us to the dockside to watch the unloading and to cadge a few nuts from the friendly dockers. When Dad worked on one we always had a bag of nuts at home. 'Hey Dad, bring us some monkey-nuts!' I yelled as he disappeared out of the door. I stuffed my pockets full whenever I went out to play, snapping open the crisp shells, tipping the nuts into my mouth and leaving a trail of shells in my wake. The nuts came from the West Indies; the oil was extracted for margarine and the residue went for animal feed.

Most families had a bowl of demerara sugar on the table for sweetening their tea, to enjoy with their breakfast porridge or sprinkle thickly on bread and butter. It was thick and sticky and ran like molten gold. But for me, the best of all was chocolate crumb. When a ship with this cargo came in the sweet smell of chocolate filled the air. It was raw chocolate, just cocoa, sugar and milk moulded into great hunks; rough-textured but with all the flavoursome taste of chocolate. It was en route to Cadburys at Bournville to be processed into the chocolate that we know. The pieces were different sizes, some just right to pop straight in and some huge and satisfying to hold and gnaw at, leaving two smooth imprints of teeth and then dissolve deliciously on the tongue. No chocolate tasted so good to me as chocolate crumb. I would watch out to see when Dad came home and if he carried a paper bag full of the lovely stuff, 'my cup runneth over'.

DAD

'Show us yer muscles, Dad,' I shouted, and he laughed as he rolled up his sleeves revealing strong hairy brown arms, but above the elbow the skin was white and smooth. He flexed his muscles and his biceps rose hard and round. 'Ooh, let me have a feel,' I said, and pressed the bulge in amazement.

Dad was a dapper chap with a moon of a face and a shock of dark hair which was brushed straight back from his forehead. Because he had short arms and legs his shirt sleeves were always too long, falling over his hands, and were kept up with armbands; a sort of fancy elastic band. 'Win, have you seen my armbands?' was often the anguished cry.

Born in 1902, Albert Edward Bennett was the youngest of a family of ten children and his brothers and sisters had doted on him. They were a close-knit family and except for an older brother, Harry, who emigrated to America when he was a young man, and Jesse, who was killed in the First World War, they all lived in Gloucestershire. Dad never moved from the street where he was born.

When just a little boy he caught diphtheria and was not expected to recover; in fact the other boy in the street that had caught it didn't survive. It left Dad with a weak throat; the quinsy, he called it, and he suffered from it a lot. He had his tonsils out, but they grew back and he had to have them taken out a second time.

He was twenty-eight years of age by the time he married Mam, but he'd had his eye on her for some time. She was only eighteen and a typical twenties flapper with short skirts and bobbed hair, with a thick fringe above hazel eyes. Dancing was her passion, especially the Charleston, so Dad had to be interested in it too to win her heart, but he gave it all up when they married. Mam was sorry that she had to give it up too as she couldn't go alone when she was a married woman, but she had loved her dancing.

She never forgot it either. Once when she was in her eighties she was at a party and some bright spark was showing off and demonstrating the Charleston. 'That's not how you do it,' said Mam, jumping up out of her chair, and she gave them all a good demonstration of the dance. She surprised everyone that she could still perform the dance of her youth.

Before she married Dad she was in service in a big house at Stinchcombe and only had one half day off each week, but Dad cycled the five or so miles to be with her. They married in 1930 and he loved her dearly all his life.

Dad was very content with his life and never wanted to go away on holiday; he worked hard and enjoyed his home. Cider was a favourite drink. Every night he went to the Railway Hotel with his bottle and it was filled with rough cider. He never stayed, just went into the Jug and Bottle for his refill, then home again and put the bottle on the floor alongside his armchair. Throughout the evening he kept on replenishing his glass until it was all gone. 'Good opening medicine my girl,' he said as his face got rosier and rosier.

He liked his cigarettes too, but moderately rolled his own and never used more than an ounce of tobacco each week; that was his ration. Many times I have been sent off on my bicycle to the nearest newsagents for an ounce of A1 tobacco and a packet of green cigarette papers. His fags were meagre affairs, not much baccy in them, and he would have to keep puffing or they would soon go out. When he put the lighted match to them there was so much spare paper on the end that a flare went up and he was in danger of singed eyebrows.

When working close to home he always came back for 'bait'. This was a midmorning break of about fifteen minutes, but Dad always managed to come home to a sit-down meal of bacon. He started work at 7.30am but never found time for breakfast, just a cup of tea, then he hurried down the road munching on a piece of bread and butter. But at ten o'clock, as regular as clockwork, he was back. 'Is my bacon ready Win?' he shouted as he flung his cap on the nearest peg. And ready it had to be; two rashers and a thick slice of bread to mop up the fat and wash it all down with a cup of tea. He sprinkled it liberally with vinegar and tucked in with relish.

Sometimes if Mam was busy I took charge of cooking his bacon and I worried about synchronising the exact time when the fat would be translucent, just as he liked it, and ready the moment he walked through the door. I would have one eye on the road to see if he was coming and another eye on the pan, willing it to be ready on time. Suitably nourished, he was off again at a trot until dinnertime.

Dad owned a set of chimney-sweeping brushes and regularly swept our chimney and anyone else's in the area that asked him. A cloth was secured over the fireplace; it had a hole in it for the rods to go through and one by one the rods were joined on to the brush, making it longer and longer until it reached right up to the top. With each push the brush rasped against the sides of the chimney and a fresh fall of soot came tumbling down. 'Run outside my girl and see if the brush is out of the chimmuck yet' he said, so out I ran and looked up expectantly. Eventually I saw the round spiky brush pop out of the top. 'It's out Dad, it's out!' I yelled, and then he began to unscrew the rods and pull the brush back down again. With each pull the soot could be heard falling thickly behind the black sheet. When he took away the sheet there was a huge pile of the stuff, which he scooped up with a shovel into a bucket and carried out, to be used on the garden at a later date. It was a dirty business and the smell of soot was everywhere.

Following 'The Sharks' was a pastime Dad enjoyed. They

were the local football team. I accompanied him whether he was watching home or away: red and white were their colours and Mam did the washing for them. There weren't any man-made easy-care fabrics then; they were of thick cotton, and every Monday Mam had a washing line full of red shirts and white shorts flapping in the breeze. I enjoyed the away matches as it meant a trip in a coach; Broadwell, Forest Green, Cinderford and Brimscombe are some of the places I remember.

Dad enjoyed listening to the music on the wireless; Tom Jenkins and his Palm Court Orchestra, Charlie Kunz playing the piano and the voice of Gracie Fields. When we sat around the fire in the evenings I would beg him for a story of times gone by.

One story was the journey he made to Uncle John's cottage at Berkeley Heath. His grandparents were dead, but his father's brother John still lived in the same cottage at Berkeley Heath. John had never married but stayed on in the cottage to look after his parents; he lived alone and when he grew old and fell ill there was no one to care for him. It was decided that the nephews should take turns in going to stay with Uncle John each night. For my father this meant a cycle ride of four or five miles after he had finished his work.

It was the middle of winter and dark when he set off to cycle along the lonely lanes from Sharpness to Berkeley Heath, and he had only gone a short way before it began to snow. As he pedalled the snow came down thicker and thicker and soon he could no longer cycle through it and was forced to dismount and push his bike. 'Bless my soul,' he said waving his arms in the air as he told his tale, 'I didn't know where I was going, I couldn't see what was road nor what was field nor 'edge.'

It was a white wilderness and the only sound was the crunching of his boots on the snow and there were no tracks but his own. There were lighted windows in the isolated cottages and the smell of wood smoke from their chimneys, but Dad felt lost and lonely and to make matters worse he was up to his knees in snow. 'I couldn't feel my feet,' he complained. But he battled on and at long last he recognised the steeple of the little church where his parents had been married and he knew he was almost there.

He pushed open the gate and made his way down the path. He reminisced about how the garden looked when he visited it when he was a boy and his grandparents were alive. It was a farm labourer's cottage, so the garden was large as they had to keep themselves supplied with fruit, vegetables and whatever else they could manage, as a farm labourer's wages were poor. It was a real cottage garden with flowers and vegetables growing together in the borders. There were fruit trees; Victoria plums and apples as big as a pudding basin, Dad said. They kept chickens for eggs and a pig at the back of the house. They also had beehives; the bees pollinated the fruit tree blossom. Once, the bees swarmed and he saw his grandmother run into the house for the frying pan. She banged it loudly on a tree to get the queen bee to alight so that the swarm could be gathered with the queen for another hive.

Grandmother always baked her own bread. She would heat up the oven by burning wood in it and when it was good and hot she raked out the ashes and put in her loaves. Dad remembered how they always had a thick, golden crust and how grandmother was in the habit of placing them on fresh cabbage leaves when they were hot; as she said, it gave them a lovely flavour.

The house was tiny, just two up and two down; just as a child would draw, with a window in each corner, a door in the middle and a chimney on the end. There was a small wash-house to the right of the door and the living room with a fireplace on the left. It was all in darkness now as Dad opened the door and went inside, as Uncle John was ill in bed. His first thought was to get a fire going and put the kettle of water on it to make a hot drink and perhaps thaw out a little and dry his clothes. He lit an oil lamp and raked the ashes out of the fireplace and rummaged around for some paper and sticks to get a good blaze going. He managed to find some knobs of coal in the lean-to outside and soon a tiny yellow flame was flickering in the grate. He eased off his wet boots and watched with satisfaction as the blaze grew bigger.

'The fire was halfway up the blummin' chimmuck' laughed Dad. He was just beginning to thaw out when he decided he had better see what kind of state that chimmuck was in, and what a shock he had as he bent down and peered up into it. Great pillows of soot several feet thick hung all around the sides and they were already beginning to glow red. Small glowing red hot pieces caught on the draught were already floating up the chimney. 'All I could see,' he said, 'was one tiny hole for the smoke to go up.'

'What did you do, Dad?' I asked in awe.

'Well, I had to put the darned thing out, I couldn't have Uncle John a burning in his bed now could I?'

So he gathered up shovelfuls of snow and dowsed the whole lovely blaze. It spluttered and hissed until it was black and dead. Poor Dad.

The cottage stayed exactly the same for years and years. No one renovated it or added anything on; it looked the same in 1993 as when my great grandparents lived there. It had a big 'For Sale' notice up and I just had to go and look at it. The last people were gone, so I was able to peer through the windows and see the fireplace that Dad talked about. The rooms were so tiny I didn't know how families survived there. As I opened the rickety gate to leave I caught the lovely scent of orange blossom as it climbing unchecked over the fence, and I plucked a piece, hoping to get it to root to remind me of the cottage where my great-grandparents had lived.

The old cottage was soon knocked down when new people bought it. Now a grand house stands on the property, with a five-barred gate and a wide sweeping drive leading to the front door.

SWIMMING

The old timber pond is inaccessible now; overgrown and a haven for all kinds of wildfowl. Lying just off the Gloucester and Berkeley Canal, it was once part of a big estate at Hinton that covered eleven acres. Sailing ships moored up there in the old days while waiting instructions for their next voyage, so it freed the docks for new arrivals. But I first heard of it listening to the grown-ups as they talked fondly of their swimming days.

'Where did you learn to swim?' asked one.

'Up the timber pond,' answered another, 'with Charlie Beard.'

'Yes, so did I,' came the reply. Charlie Beard was a local man well known for teaching the young people to swim.

And so they chattered on about their swimming days and I never grew tired of listening to them. It sounded a magical place to me and I wanted to be part of it. I never visited it, or even saw it. Once when travelling on the canal I asked my father, 'Where's the timber pond then Dad?'

'Oh, over there behind them trees,' he answered with a brief wave of his arm. But peer as I might to see through the trees or crane my neck to see over them it was all hidden from my view. And so it always seemed magical to me, a bit like still-wrapped presents under the Christmas tree.

There was no mixed bathing then; the girls went on one evening and the boys on another. They were rowed out to the middle of the pond, where it was deepest, and with a rope securely tied around their waist and someone holding tight to the other end, they were made to jump in. When they could swim they were allowed to go on their own, and Auntie Ivy told me how she would rush home from school on a sunny day, slice a 'knobby' off a loaf of bread, cut some onion and cheese and wrap the lot in newspaper. With that tucked under her arm she made for the dusty red path that ran alongside the canal and pushed her way through hawthorn, bramble and dog rose bushes until she came to a clearing and the timber pond was waiting for her. After a refreshing swim she unwrapped the newspaper and enjoyed her tea.

When the track became too overgrown, the young people wanting to swim were ferried to the timber pond in a rowing boat along the canal, which must have been a treat in itself. Eventually it was too overgrown to reach it at all. The old dock was no longer in use by then, so the young people were taken there to learn to swim. This was where my mother was taught and with the rope around her waist she was taken to an old barge and made to jump into the water. I couldn't imagine what it must have felt like.

'Oh, I was frightened,' Mam said when I asked her. 'It was very dark and cold and I sank down and down for what seemed like forever. And then I felt a tug on my waist and I slowly resurfaced.' She was able to swim within a week.

But in the 1940s we had no such supervision. We were left to our own devices. Some swam in the Severn, but the canal was nearer to me, so that was my watering hole. It was a popular meeting place and as soon as we had a few days of warm weather young people could be seen with rolled-up towels tucked under their arms making their way along the railway track which led to the bathing spot. Dog roses and bramble were in blossom and straying branches snatched at us as we pushed our way through and crunched along the red, gravelly path. Finally we came to a clearing which we called First Bay; if it was too crowded you could push on through the bushes to another bay or on to a third. These bays were formed by the swell of water from the tugs, barges and tankers which ploughed up and down the canal; it constantly washed the banks and, over the years, had eroded the soft red sandstone. In between the bays were little rocky outcrops, often with bushes or trees growing on them.

As we greeted our friends, boys larked about and chased each other, flipping their towels at bare legs, shouting and yelling as they went. The bushes were useful to hide behind while changing into our swimsuits and little piles of clothing were dotted about all over the bank. The sharp red rock was awkward to climb down; it was gritty to stand on and uncomfortable to tender skin. As you waded out there would suddenly be a sharp drop where sandstone had worn away, leaving a shelf of rock. When the tugs ploughed up and down, the *Addie, Primrose, Mayflower, Iris* or *Stanegarth,* we shouted and waved to the crew, then sat down and waited for the swell. The waves lapped right over us and then receded, dragging the red grit with a rasping sound and exposing those dangerous ledges that I feared so much.

The old Severn Bridge was close by, one end at Sharpness and the other in Blakeney in the Forest of Dean. It was a beautiful railway bridge of 21 huge spans; built in 1879 it was 4,162 feet in length and used to bring coal from the Forest to be taken on up into the Midlands. It was also a line for a steam passenger train to take children to Lydney Grammar School, and local people enjoyed it too for travelling to Lydney to shop for items that couldn't be bought at Sharpness. Mam went regularly and brought back fresh fish. Fish was not rationed during the war, but we couldn't get any at Sharpness. The fish was wrapped in paper, so whatever else she brought in her bag also smelt of fish. She often brought back currant buns, so these had a fishy taste too, and a book she bought me once had a fishy smell every time I turned a page.

Sometimes, as a treat, I went with Mam, Auntie Phyllis and my cousins to a lovely park where there were swings and a roundabout. The park was large, with huge oak trees which had hollowed-out trunks; great places to hide. It was part of a large estate given to the people of Lydney by the wealthy landowner. It was a lovely place to play. We took a picnic and there was a drinking fountain with a cup made of very thick metal fixed on with a stout chain; I remember the feel of the thick, cold metal against my mouth as I gulped the fresh, cold water. I wonder if it is still there.

The train always stopped just over the bridge, at the station there, and I used to look down to the sands far below where the people looked just like ants running about. We went just over the bridge once and got off at Blakeney. Dad worked with Jeff Protheroe, who came from there, and said if Mam went over we could have some plums as there was a glut of them that year; we could have as many as we liked. As my youngest brother was a baby we took the pram in the guard's van and got off the train at Blakeney .

Dad had told Mam how to get to Jeff Protheroe's house, saying it wasn't far. But Mam had no sense of direction and took a wrong turning and we went up hill and down dale for what seemed like hours. Henry, who was three years older than me, complained loudly he was tired. But so was Mam, and she was cross having to push the pram. 'You just shut up or I'll throw you over that hedge!' she threatened.

At last we found the cottage and the lovely garden full of heavily-laden plum trees. 'Oh,' exclaimed Mrs Protheroe to her daughter when Mam told her the way we had come, 'they bin all up round Carter's farm and back that way.' She fetched us some cold water to drink and we filled the pram up with plums. After a rest we set out for the station and went the right way that time; it was only a hop, skip and a jump and we were there.

We enjoyed watching the train going across when we were swimming and always waved madly to the passengers, knowing we must have looked like ants to them.

The older children who went to the grammar school had learned to swim proficiently and would show their skill by diving off the rocky outcrops. They swam right across the canal, got out on to the towpath, which separated the canal from the Severn, climbed over the low wall and disappeared. I thought them very brave, especially as the Severn is notorious for its dangerous quicksand; I longed to be able to do it. After a while they came back covered from head to foot in Severn mud and dragging seaweed while they danced along the towpath like minstrels with the mud drying and cracking on their bodies before swimming back across the canal.

As summer came to an end, our trips to the canal bank became fewer. We had paced ourselves on the sleepers between the railway lines which led to it, with our swimsuits and towels tucked under our arm, for the last time. No more picnics with blackberry jam sandwiches and the bread stained purple. The black and yellow caterpillars that we had watched munching on the ragwort had turned into cinnabar moths with paper-thin red and black wings and flown away. The snow-white blossom of May had changed into rich, red haws; the delicate dog roses had gone and now jewel-like hips hung from every branch; and the brambles that had snatched at our clothes were now heavy with blackberries, ripe for picking and making into jam for next year.

The bank was deserted. We walked away, then turned for one last look at the inviting water and listened as it lapped and dragged at the red grit. We would be back next summer.

THE PEN

At the end of the street, through an archway formed by a high road going over it, was an area of pasture. Dad rented part of it from the Dock Company for a smallholding. It was always known as the Pen. It covered about an acre and consisted of a yard with a hotchpotch of wooden buildings; hen coops, pig sties, a shed for the goats, and a pigeon loft as well a large vegetable garden with apple and plum trees. And a stretch of pasture, which was not very wide but long; it ran right down to the canal and abounded with primroses, violets and cowslips in spring and dog roses in the summer.

We always had chickens, ducks and geese, which provided us with eggs and meat during the austere war years. The old gander knew I was scared of him and always stretched out his neck and rushed at me, hissing violently whenever he saw me coming.

Mam kept goats, and Trixie and Gertie were the first ones she bought. They followed her everywhere, bleating as they went. Once a day she led them to their shed and hooked their collars onto a nail to keep them still. She pulled up a stool and reached for an old navy beret which was kept hanging up on a nail and pulled it over her hair to keep it clean and free from any goaty smell. The goats chewed their cud contentedly while Mam talked and soothed them, then with her head against their flank the milk was soon pinging into the pail. She strained it through some muslin while the cats rubbed around her legs hoping for their share, and she handed a cupful to me to drink; it was warm and sweet and nutty.

The goats didn't need to produce kids every year to supply milk. They would go on giving milk for several years, but eventually it would get less and less and they would need to be in kid again. Mam bought a billy goat once, but you could smell it for miles, so she didn't keep it long, but we had several little kids born.

When the milk was plentiful she made cream and butter by whisking the milk in a bowl. This was all done by hand, so it took a while to turn and a lot of hard work by Mam. When it turned into butter she washed it in fresh cold water, put it into a muslin cloth and squeezed it to remove any remaining buttermilk. She patted the white butter into a neat square and it tasted fresh and good. Buttermilk was used for making scones and soda bread and any not needed went to the pigs.

The goats were tethered on any grass on the dock and Dad, in the autumn, cut the long grass with a scythe and let it dry into hay for winter feed. If Mam looked out of the window and saw it was raining, she would hurry down the street and take the goats to their shed, as they hated being out in the rain.

Once, when one goat had reached the end of its life, Mam made a rug from its hide, but having cured it herself it was stiff and hard, not supple as it should have been. But it graced the floor in front of her dressing table in the bedroom for many years.

Dad had a loft of racing pigeons. You had to climb up some wooden steps to get into it and often I was cajoled into cleaning it out on a Saturday afternoon. The mess from the pigeons on the floor and perches was hard to scrape off and smelly too, and all the while the pigeons flapped about my ears as I worked.

Saturday afternoon was also the time I sat with him eagerly scanning the sky waiting for the pigeons to return home. The day before he had taken them to the local railway station in a basket and they had travelled up north by train, with others from the area, and were all released at a specific time. We waited for the first one home. 'There he is!' shouted Dad in excitement. 'Here he comes, mind now don't frighten him, let him go in.' Once the bird was safely in the loft, Dad removed a tag and we hot-footed it up to the Railway Hotel, where, at the back, there was a room specially for the pigeon fanciers. Dad pushed the tag into a box, a bit like a clocking-on box, which recorded the time the bird arrived home. Then it was back to the pen to await the others. Dad won a silver cup for his pigeon racing.

We always had a pig in the sty, fed on scraps and pig meal. There was a dockers' canteen not far away and Dad was allowed to collect all the left-over food. He cycled there and came home with a bucket on each handlebar full of food and peelings at the end of each day. Mam scoffed at the thin potato peelings. 'They do use one of them peelers I do reckon,' she said. Mam always peeled her potatoes thickly with a sharp knife. We had a very old chaffing machine with a handle and a blade on a wheel; the straw was fed in and when the handle was turned it made a satisfying scrunch as it sliced the straw for the pig's bed.

When the pig was fat enough, the day came for it to be killed. Fred Watts was called. He had a humane gun which he put to the pig's forehead and the pig dropped dead instantly. Fred was called when anyone wanted old dogs put to sleep, and he also castrated all the tomcats in the area. Fred always went home with the choicest joint of pork from the pig for his trouble.

Friends could be relied upon to help out after a pig was killed, to scrub it down and singe off whiskers, and they were given some meat too. Mam used all of the pig; there were no refrigerators then, so she had to get on with it. She made faggots from the offal, cleaned the gut for chitterlings and made brawn from the head. She used the trotters too, which were boiled on the fire till they were soft as jelly, and we lived like lords for a while. The hams were boiled and the sides of the pig were cured into bacon at home using saltpetre (potassium nitrate). This had to be well rubbed in over a period of several weeks and the great flitches were hung in the larder. The resulting bacon was dry, hard and salty, but Mam sliced off thick rashers with a bone-handled carving knife for Dad's bait and he thought it was the best ever. Even the bladder of the pig was blown up and used as a football; it was surprisingly tough when dried and we had fun kicking it up and down the street.

Dad had an incubator for hatching chickens. It was kept in a shed in the garden at home so he could keep an eye on it, as the temperature had to be constant. It was like a large wooden cabinet with about six or seven drawers along the width of it where the eggs were set in rows. A gentle heat was provided by a paraffin heater in the base, and every day Dad pulled open the drawers and turned the eggs as a mother hen would have done naturally. Eventually the drawers were opened and revealed chicks in different stages of hatching; some already dry, fluffy and cheeping, some still damp, having just emerged from the shell, and some still inside with their little beaks pecking away at the shell in the struggle to get out.

The hatched ones were removed from the incubator to another shed where there was a heater like an old paraffin lamp but with a round metal dome to hold the lighted wick. The chicks ran about, fed and scratched until they were big enough to go down the pen.

Dad always took a paper called *The Smallholder*, and he ordered the eggs from an advertisement. They arrived by rail and we fetched them from the station. They were packed in strong hexagonal boxes, holding a dozen eggs in each, and Mam sometimes made use of the boxes by creating them into attractive containers for needlework. She covered them in silk brocade and padded the insides; the top, too, was covered and with a few reels of cotton, some needles and scissors inside they made attractive Christmas presents.

When I was about ten years of age Dad decided to get a pony for my brother and me to ride. We had the long strip of pasture, so Dad set about building a stable at the one end adjoining the pen. He kept a lookout in the Gazette, the local paper, to look for any suitable ponies, and eventually Bridget arrived. She was a brown Welsh cob, sturdy and quiet but stubborn too. When I had learnt to ride well enough to set off on my own through the local villages it was a battle of wills to get her to go. As we got to the High Road and were leaving the Pen behind us she suddenly dug her heels in and refused to budge. She tossed her head and showed the whites of her eyes and the only way she would go was home.

I gripped her with my knees and urged her forward. 'Go on Bridget, go on!' I said, but she just turned and faced home. This continued for several minutes with us doing circles in the middle of the road, but eventually I got the better of her and we trotted off the way I wanted to go.

On returning home Dad always asked the same question, 'How did she go?' My answer was always the same, too – 'She didn't half go coming back.' Dad walked away laughing and repeating my answer to himself.

He entered me in a couple of local shows, but I never won anything; I was no match for the farmers' daughters. Their ponies were better than mine and they had been riding all their lives.

Mam had to get me some jodhpurs, as wearing my slacks chafed the insides of my legs. Clothes were still hard to come by and needed coupons even if they were available, so again the Gazette came to our rescue when Mam saw some second-hand ones advertised. They were beige corduroy and fitted perfectly, but being second hand I suppose I looked down on them a bit. I wanted to knit myself a jumper to go with them and we had some yellow wool, but not quite enough. Mam found some matching silky thread and suggested that I use it by knitting two rows of silk and four rows of wool. It worked well and made an attractive jumper to wear for riding.

Out cantering on the green one day, I heard galloping hooves behind me and riding towards me was a girl of about my age, although I didn't know her well as she was educated privately. She was the daughter of the local shipping magnate and a grand yacht in the dock, *Diana Mary*, was named after her. but she was friendly and pleased to see me. She spotted my jodhpurs and said, 'Oh, corduroy jodhpurs, you lucky thing!' so I felt better about them after that. We swopped ponies for a ride; hers was smaller, quicker and much more willing than Bridget. We set off like a rocket with hardly any urging from me, very different to stubborn Bridget; I had to cling on tightly.

Dad decided to let Bridget have a foal, so we took her to a stud at Stroud and left her there for a while. She must have been keen, because the owner told us how she had swum across a stretch of water to get to the horses on the other side. Anyway she was in foal and my riding had to be curbed for a bit. The new foal had already been born when Dad went down the pen one morning. Years before Mam and Dad had had a golden cocker spaniel named Julie. They had thought the world of her, and Dad said the new foal had been born on the exact spot where Julie was buried, so Julie was the name of Bridget's daughter.

Julie was lighter in colour than her mother, sort of gingery, and much more highly strung; she pranced and shook her head, showing her aristocracy. When she was broken in Henry and I could go off riding together. We went hunting once but kept well behind, just enjoying the gallop over farmers' fields.

The next thing Dad bought was a governess cart, a pretty two-wheeled gig. It had a little door at the back with a fancy iron step to help you get in and two seats facing each other, padded and covered in real leather. Bridget went well between the shafts and we had many rides around the pretty country lanes.

Once Henry and I thought we would go a bit further afield and decided on Shepperdine, which is on the Severn down towards Bristol. It can be seen from Sharpness as a point of land jutting into the Severn about seven miles away. We packed some sandwiches for our lunch and set off. There were hardly any cars on the road then and it was pleasant trotting along the country lanes with just the sound of the pony's hooves. The fresh green trees almost met above us, creating a shady tunnel, the scent of elderberry blossom was all around us and the verges bright with moon daisies and cow parsley. But we were only just through Berkeley and heading towards Ham when we both looked at each other and decided we were hungry, so out came our peanut butter sandwiches and we ate the lot as we jogged along. But we still made it to Shepperdine and back; it took about two hours each way.

The trap was useful for our haymaking. In the autumn Dad was able to gather up cut grass from around the dock for winter feed. He cut it all by hand with a scythe and left it to dry. Then we raked it up into heaps with wide wooden rakes, and with pitchforks we piled it high on the little trap. On the homeward journey I perched on top of it all to hold it down and it swung violently over bumps or round corners, but I surveyed the world from new heights and felt I was king of the castle.

Dad loved his pen; it was his life. And Mam too; she always shared the duties. They were familiar figures walking up and down the street several times a day with a galvanised bucket on their arm with grain in for the chickens or some pig food. Or on the way back a few eggs nestled on straw or vegetables for the table. And always with a dog at their heels; usually a black and white collie. There was Tim, then Bess and later Jessie. Jessie always took herself off for a swim in the canal, then struck off across the fields hunting rabbits. She was gone for a couple of hours sometimes. We all enjoyed the good life.

ELVERS

Elvers are a delicacy now and are on the endangered species list. A licence is needed to fish for them and the river police patrol the banks to catch anyone fishing illegally. Most are sent to fish farms out east, Europe and Asia, where they are sold for the table or used for restocking. They can fetch as much as £300 per kilo.

But when I was a child, elvers made a cheap meal. In early spring, February or March, Sharpness folk began to think about elvers and look forward to their first meal of them and so you would catch snatches of conversation. 'Bit too cold ennit Frank, fer elvers just yet?'

'Ah, tis you, they won't be up yet awhile' came the reply. The weather had to be warm enough for elvers.

Elvers (glass eels was another name for them) were about two inches long with thread-like bodies that looked like spun glass. A black line ran along their backs and they had black eyes. They had worked their way up the warm Gulf Stream from their spawning grounds in the Sargasso Sea, taking two or three years to reach us. When the temperature was right, millions of the little creatures pushed their way up the River Severn and were swept into the docks with the tide. Local people gathered at the side of the basin and peered into it with their homemade nets poised and galvanised buckets at the ready for their catch. The basin is the part of the dock between lock gates where water is pumped in or out to allow ships to pass through, and when the water receded elvers clung to the sides in a writhing mass, just waiting to be scooped up. The nets, usually made from an old gauze meat cover wired on to a wooden frame then secured to a bamboo pole handle, were dragged along the basin wall, then hauled up and the contents tipped into the waiting buckets, which soon filled up, and I gazed in at the seething, wriggling jumble of baby eels.

Anyone could try their hand at elver fishing in those days and boys would rush home from school and join in, then sell their wares for sixpence a pound to make some extra pocket money. For a while everyone in Sharpness would have their fill of elvers. If relations happened to be visiting, real townie types, they would peer into the galvanised buckets aghast and say, 'you're not eating them are you? Well, I thought at least they would be in a white pail.'

The elvers had to be thoroughly cleaned before they were ready for the table. They were tipped into a cotton bag with a handful of salt and plenty of fresh water was sloshed on them; then the bag was squeezed, exuding a glutinous frothy mass, and this had to be repeated several times until they were clean and free from slime.

In Jane Grigson's book *English Food*, she says the way to cook elvers is to fry them in bacon fat until they are opaque, pour over some beaten egg, cook for a few more minutes, then serve them very hot. Dad liked his fried in bacon fat, sprinkled with plenty of salt and vinegar and served up with a rasher of bacon, and he enjoyed them with bread and butter. Every year we had the same routine. I knew what was coming – he always tried to get me to join him. 'Come on our Joyce,' he would say, 'have a taste, they're lovely.' He would gather up a forkful from his plate, twirling them around like spaghetti, then I would lean towards the proffered forkful, not really wanting them but not wanting to offend him, so I took them gingerly between my teeth. The salty, vinegary taste attacked my senses first, then they felt like bits of string on my tongue. I rolled them around my mouth, then began to chew. They did not have an unpleasant flavour but felt gritty as I bit into them and I imagined it was their eyes. Dad always watched expectantly as I swallowed, but I pulled a face and spluttered, 'No more Dad, I don't want any more.'

When the elvers begin to darken in colour they are considered over their best and are left to continue their journey to streams, ponds or ditches, where they stay for as long as eight or nine years, growing into eels. Then they make their long trek back to the place of their birth, where they spawn and die.

Dad always liked to tell a tale about Mam when she was a young, new housewife. She had decided to cook him a feast of elvers for his tea and, although we don't like the thought of it today, they were usually cooked while still alive, as you knew they were fresh then. Mam scooped the wriggling mass into a cold pan with a knob of fat, but didn't put a lid on the pan as she should have done. She left the kitchen for a few minutes and what a sight met her eyes when she returned to see how they were getting on. Well, they might have looked fragile creatures but they had found super strength.

'You never saw anything like it in your life,' laughed Dad. 'The little blighters were everywhere, slithering down the stove, all over the floor, even up the walls to the ceiling.' Poor Mam, she never lived it down. 'We were picking off dried elvers for weeks afterwards,' laughed Dad.

THE PLANTATION

The Plantation was magical. Other names for it were the Old Pleasure Grounds or the Point, and Dad always spoke of 'over on the Point'.

The Plantation was an island. It was a high piece of land jutting into the River Severn and it was bordered by the Severn and the dock, but despite being close to a busy working dock it was a place of tranquillity and was used for celebrating important occasions such as coronations, jubilees and Sunday school treats.

It was used in 1879 after the opening of the Severn Bridge, which linked Sharpness with the Forest of Dean by rail, when the Committee and Officials 'retired to the Pleasure Grounds for a celebratory tea'. Just mention the Plantation to the older folk in Sharpness today and their faces will crinkle into a smile as they remember it with fondness.

The house of white stucco at the entrance to the Plantation was once a fishing lodge for the Lords of Berkeley. Later, when it was privately owned, the residents charged a small entrance fee for people to walk in the Plantation, served refreshments and also rented it out for celebrations. Pleasure boats called steam packets brought parties down the canal from Gloucester to enjoy the Plantation.

The Severn was about a mile wide at that point and there were lovely views over it to the Forest of Dean with trees of all shades of green everywhere. But each autumn their red and tawny orange tints made them look as if they were ablaze.

A well-worn path led to a secluded beach where there were caves which had formed where the tide had eroded away the soft red sandstone. When the new dock was being built the caves were used for storing the dynamite that was needed to blast the flint-hard rock for sinking in the shafts of the new pier.

A path led down towards the old dock, which was quiet and still now but complete with all its trappings. Swans nested in half-sunken barges and the Harbourmaster's house, white and with an important-looking porticoed porch, stood alone at the entrance near the Basin. Beyond that were vast swathes of the Severn and you could see Blakeney and the Forest of Dean. Lock gates, bollards, ropes and chains were all evidence of the busy dock it had once been. Old red brick buildings where the horses used to be stabled still sat squarely near the towpath. Horses were used for towing barges along the canal or for pulling cargo from the dock up through the Plantation to waiting lorries and trucks, to continue its way by road or rail on up into the Midlands.

A towpath leading to Purton and beyond was a pleasant walk on a Sunday afternoon. A thick, sturdy, low wall covered in lichen and about knee high separated the dock and the canal from the Severn, and over the wall was the vast expanse of the treacherous sinking sands of the river. Not far away was the Severn railway bridge. The old dock was a small sheltered little harbour and I tried to imagine Sharpness before the new dock, before all the silos, warehouses, timber sheds, rows of houses and shops were built. It was just fields and tracks, this little harbour and beautiful views across the Severn.

All the time I was growing up at Sharpness there was a training ship named the *Vindicatrix* moored in the Old Dock. She was towed to Sharpness in 1939 from Gravesend because it was safer at Sharpness during the war. The ship stayed at Sharpness for twenty-eight years and was the headquarters of the National Sea Training School. A new intake of the lads came by train to Sharpness railway station every Friday and I watched them make their way to the *Vindicatrix*, where they stayed for training; 'Vindi boys', as they were known, were a familiar sight in their navy uniform walking from their ship to the Seaman's Mission at the other end of the dock.

The Plantation was dark and tranquil, with a labyrinth of mossy paths and canopied with trees of elm, oak and ash. Here and there among the trees were seats, made by cutting an old rowing boat in half and upending it with the point in the air; it made a delightful shelter to sit in for a chat and observe the scene. Old railway carriages no longer needed had been gutted and set among the trees, and at celebratory teatimes women could be seen inside preparing plates of sandwiches and urns of tea.

Hidden away among the trees and marked by a swarm of

buzzing flies so you always knew when you were near, was a shack, and inside was a wooden seat with a hole in the middle and a bucket below. No one went too close unless they had to.

The Plantation was always the rendezvous for our Sunday School treats. We had to attend Sunday school all year to qualify and we walked the mile to chapel each Sunday afternoon dressed in our best clothes and clutching our penny collection tightly. Any silver paper we had managed to save from chocolate was pushed into a box just inside the door. Then we made our way into the back room and sat on little varnished chairs. As we gave up our pennies we sang:

> *Dropping, dropping, dropping,*
> *Hear the pennies fall,*
> *Every one for Jesus,*
> *The Lord God loves us all.*

'Mam, Mam hurry up and do my hair,' I wailed, hopping from one leg to the other. 'They'll be going without me.'

'No they won't,' Mam reassured me as she ran the comb along to get a straight parting and scooped up a handful of hair to tie on my yellow satin ribbon in a floppy bow. 'There's plenty of time.'

It was the day I had been waiting for. I had trudged to Sunday school every Sunday and I didn't intend to miss a moment of it. I was already decked out in my finery, a yellow silk dress decorated with tiny pink rosebuds, and I was anxious to be off.

Henry, three years older than me, was in the kitchen dabbing water on his hair; he had a 'cow's lick' and tried to make it lie flat. Mam tied his stripey knitted tie and checked him over. His red and black belt fastened with an S-shaped buckle and I always admired it and wanted one.

'Have you both got clean hankies?' asked Mam. We were in a state of wild excitement and the tension was getting too much. Henry pulled my sash undone, then stuck out his foot so that I went flying. 'Mam, Mam!' I yelled.

'You shut up, our Joyce!' Henry warned, 'or I'll give you the Chinese Burn.' This was a method of torture he threatened me with, when he would rub my skin fast and hard with his knuckles till it burned; usually on the back of my neck. 'You behave yourselves, the pair of you,' came Mam's exasperated voice. 'Or you'll feel my hand on your backsides and be sent upstairs to bed.'

Duly admonished, we set off on the mile walk to Newtown. We all gathered outside the chapel, everyone dressed in their Sunday best. The Sharpness Silver Band led the procession and the men looked very smart in their uniforms and the silver instruments sparkled in the sunshine. We jostled for best position, as two children were always elected to carry the banner which was held aloft in all its orange glory with the words 'The Good Shepherd' emblazoned in gold. As it was about a mile to walk the little children were given a ride in a horse and cart. So we began our journey heralded by loud music, and all the way along the road people came to their doorways to watch and wave us on.

We paraded up the New Road, turned left at the Railway Hotel, went across the viaduct, then over the High Bridge which spanned the canal and we were nearly there. Our excitement rose as we crunched along the gravel path with the Plantation in sight. The clatter of crockery from the railway carriages met our ears and set out under the trees were the trestle tables all laid with starchy white tablecloths. The trees were decorated with bunting wound around and around the trunks, and lanterns hung from branches.

As soon as we were able, we broke ranks and scampered off among the trees, glad to be free. It was cool and dark with shafts of sunlight piercing the branches, and a damp, earthy scent filled the air as our feet pounded the mossy paths. Rope swings hung from some of the lower branches and planks placed on fallen tree-trunks made ideal seesaws.

'I'll race you to the swings!' I shouted as we ran off. We hid in the tall ferns and ran to peer over the edge at the Severn below us.

We had the usual races; egg and spoon, three-legged race and a slow bicycle race where the winner was the one who came last, so the riders wobbled and zigzagged, trying not to fall off. Eventually we took our seats at the tables and after grace was said we tucked in while huge white enamel jugs full of hot, sweet tea were brought around to wash it all down. A lady in a white apron came out of the house with a big bowl of home-made ice cream which was spooned into our dishes, creamy and delicious. At the end of the afternoon someone always appeared with a tin of toffees and threw handfuls into the air while we scrambled for them shouting with glee and grabbing as many as we could. The end to a perfect day.

Then it was the turn of the grown-ups. The band played popular tunes of the day while couples danced under the trees. If there were ships in dock then the sailors came and joined in too. But for us youngsters the fun was over for another year and we were bundled off home to bed to dream of delicious ice cream and toffees spinning through the air.

THE ENTERTAINER

Dad looked like Arthur Askey – people often commented on it. But the similarity didn't end there; he liked to entertain too. He never had any music lessons and wouldn't have known what a crotchet or a quaver was if you asked him, but he could get a tune out of anything. The thing most people remembered him for was his clappers, or bones as they used to be called, probably because they were made of bone many years ago. Dad's were of hard, black ebony, about seven inches long, an inch and a half wide and three eighths of an inch thick. He held two in each hand between the fingers; one between his forefinger and middle finger and the other between his middle and ring finger.

'Play us your clappers Dad,' I begged, and he put the wireless on, as we had no other means of music, and started to play. The sound that came as he shook his hands was loud and clear and satisfying. His whole body shook to the music as he rolled his arms in front then up over his head and then behind him all the while he clicked and clacked like a Spanish señorita's castanets. His blue eyes twinkled and his smiling face got more and more rosy.

'Do it again Dad, do it again!' I begged when he had finished and with a flourish we were treated to another performance with more gusto.

Dad was nimble on his feet and he was a dab hand at the Cobblers, a Russian dance, which was very difficult to do, where he squat on his haunches, folded his arms in front and kicked out his feet to the music. Even in his forties he could still entertain us with the Cobblers. I tried it and it made my legs ache so much I couldn't keep it up for long.

He played the piano by ear. He had never had any lessons, while I went every week along to Mrs Griffey who lived nearby and put my sixpence on her red plush tablecloth for my weekly lesson. I practised hard with my crotchets, quavers and minims but Dad could beat me. He picked out the tune with the right hand and just vamped with the left, playing popular tunes of the day: *Lily of Laguna* or *Ain't She Sweet*. I envied him and wanted to be able to play like it.

He liked to have friends in sometimes for a musical get-together. A group of them would gather in our living room; Uncle Dave with his accordion, Cyril Savage with his mandolin and someone with a kettle drum. Dad stocked up with cider to 'wet their whistles' and in between tunes would call, 'Have another one Dave, drink up Cyril.' As the evening wore on they all became merrier, their faces rosier and the music louder until our house was fair reverberating with the sound.

Dad could get music out of anything; a comb and paper, mouth organ or a Jew's harp. This was a small lyre-shaped musical instrument with a tongue of spring steel; you held it between your teeth and twanged at the metal tongue, and you could get different notes out of it as you altered the shape of your mouth.

About a mile away, in New Street at Newtown, was a parish room which was used for all kinds of entertainment; dances, parties and concerts. It had a stage with curtains and a dressing room and for concerts rows of wooden chairs were set in place. There were travelling troupes which used to come and these were always looked forward to eagerly. But sometimes local people put on their own concert. There were always baritones, sopranos or pianists willing to do a turn. Will Nash sang *John Brown's body lies a-mouldering in the grave* and Bill Peart gave us a monologue called 'My Meatless Day'.

I too had been on that stage. Someone began a tap and ballet dancing class. The lessons were held in a room at the back of the chapel; the same room where I attended Sunday School. My cousin Phyllis played the piano to accompany the dancers. I went avidly and learnt simple tap and ballet movements. Mam bought me some gold, strappy sandals and Dad took me to the cobblers to have steel pieces added on to the toes and heels to make the tapping sound.

As we progressed we danced in groups of three or more. At one practice I had lent my sandals to a friend for the weekend as she was to be a bridesmaid and didn't have any pretty shoes of her own. As we went through our dance routine I got to one point and went wrong. We started again from the beginning, but the same thing happened; the dance was interrupted with my wrong steps. 'Perhaps it's because you haven't got your proper dancing shoes,' said the teacher, 'see if someone will lend you theirs.' I borrowed some my size and went straight through the routine with no problem.

When we were thought to be proficient enough, a concert of our dancing was arranged in the parish room. Clothes and fabrics were still in short supply just after the war, so yards and yards of cotton muslin was purchased and dyed to the appropriate shades. Mam dyed mine pale green and pink as I was dancing to the music *Country Gardens* by Percy Grainger. The skirt was made up of layer upon layer of petal-shaped pieces which floated prettily as we danced. I expect all the mothers were proud.

Dad used to tell us about his turn on the stage. It was the story of the wooden doll. It was a turn he did when he was younger with a puppet but minus its head. It measured about eighteen inches and was dressed in smart red check jacket and blue trousers. The legs were jointed and at the back of the knees a handle was fixed so that the doll could be made to dance. The doll was fixed around Dad's neck, hiding the join with a big bow of red ribbon so Dad's head became the head of the doll. It had its own little stage and curtains and a table top to dance on and Dad just put his head through the curtain so that his moon of a face and the doll's little body were all the audience could see.

'Well,' said Dad, 'when they pulled back the main curtains, talk about laugh. It was ages before I could begin. They were all roaring with laughter and then when I moved a little leg – well it brought the house down.' It was a huge success; the doll completed its turn with a tap dance to rapturous applause and calls of, 'Encore, Encore'. I wish I had been there.

WAR

I was five years old when World War Two began. I have strong recollections of being carried by Mam to Policeman Smith's house on that day. Policeman Smith lived nearby in the street but in a bigger house than ours, and as we were not in the habit of going to his house it has stuck in my memory. We all went to listen to his wireless and the important announcement by Baldwin on the 11th of September 1939 to say that we were at war with Germany. Either we didn't own a wireless then or the accumulator needed changing. A man came once a fortnight to swop over accumulators, taking the old one back for recharging.

As my mother carried me with my hand over her shoulder I ran my fingers up and down the stitching on the back of her dark blue coat. It was like the rungs of a ladder; a row of tucks in the fabric: clothes in the 20s and 30s were often adorned with tucks, darts and ruching.

Food rationing affected Mam more than it did me. I was well

fed, except for sweets. I was always plaguing Mam for a ha'penny to get some sweeties. When rationing came in I had an understanding with Dad that he could have my bacon ration if I could have his sweet coupons. That suited us both.

We made sweets at home sometimes, especially toffee if the rations stretched to it; it was chewy, real stick-jaw stuff. And also some chocolate fudge rolled into balls and tossed in cocoa, but they weren't very good. Sometimes for a treat we mixed cocoa and sugar in a cup and wetted our finger and dipped it in to suck at. It was better than nothing.

We each had our own ration book as well as identity cards with our own registration number on, which had to be carried around with us at all times. The pages of the ration books were marked into squares for different dates. When we collected our ration for that week the appropriate square was crossed through. There was a points system for things like tinned fruit or salmon; a certain number of points were allowed each month and these were cut out as you used them. Tiny squares of paper were passed across the counter. Rations for each person each week were two ounces of cheese, four ounces of margarine, two ounces of butter, eight ounces of sugar, two ounces of tea, plus one pound of jam every two months and three ounces of sweets each month. You got one fresh egg each week if available, but sometimes only one every two weeks.

Mam hated dried egg. It came in a cardboard box and looked like yellow powder, a bit like dried mustard powder. The instructions told you how much to use in place of a whole egg.

Omelettes made with it were flat and like leather; nothing like the fluffy ones made with fresh eggs. But it wasn't too bad for cakes. Most of the time we had our own fresh eggs, but in winter the chickens didn't lay so many so Mam used to preserve some. She put them into a bucket then poured over something called isinglass which she had mixed with water. Isinglass is a form of gelatin obtained from fish and it formed a coating on the porous eggshell and stopped the egg from going bad. They were better than dried eggs, but not so good as fresh ones.

Dad always killed a cockerel for our Christmas dinner. It was something to look forward to as chicken was too expensive then to have at any other time. If we had fresh pork or cured bacon from our own pig we had to hand in the meat coupons. We weren't allowed to have both.

Our food was simple; porridge for breakfast with syrup and toast with peanut butter. Usually we had some kind of meat and two veg for dinner. Dad complained about the sausages – 'They be vull of sawdust,' he moaned. They were padded out with a lot more cereal than meat. Spam was sliced and dipped in batter to make it go further, and Mam made fish and chips sometimes and homemade soup from a few bones and lots of vegetables; it simmered away on the open fire. And there was Woolton Pie, with lots of root vegetables. Carrots, parsnips and swedes were chopped up and put in a dish, then a gravy flavoured with Marmite was poured over and the whole thing was covered with pastry, sometimes with oatmeal added to give more goodness. The Ministry of Food sent out leaflets advising people how to eat more nourishingly and a Mr Woolton had made up the recipe for the pie so it was named after him. But it was never a favourite.

Mam was not a very imaginative cook; there were never any savoury rice dishes. 'Rice is for puddings,' she said. When I had my own home and cookery books I was surprised to see recipes for curries and sweet and sour or garlic mentioned. I thought it was something new come from India, not realising that people had always eaten it, because we never had it at home. And we never ate out as there were no restaurants nearby, just tearooms for the dockers. If we went to Gloucester it was a treat to be taken to Lane's fish and chip shop for our lunch.

We only had pudding on a Sunday, when it was usually a fruit tart; rhubarb, plum or apple, served with custard, or to Dad's delight with tinned condensed milk. 'Let's 'ave another spoonful of that milk, Win, this rhubarb's a bit tangy' he would say. In fact, when the war was over and we had real cream with tinned fruit, Dad whined, 'Can't we ave some 'o that proper cream Win, out of a tin!'

I loved it too. I thought to myself, 'When I'm earning my own money I shall buy loads of condensed milk.' But I never did, because I was adult then and had lost my taste for it. Shame!

We only had fruit when it was in season. Plums were really cheap; 2d a pound, if there was a glut and we had our own apple trees down the pen. One apple tree was a Blenheim and Dad was proud of them. They were huge; he picked them in their prime and stored them in the back bedroom spread out over the floor. No one was allowed to try one before Christmas as he thought they had mellowed and were at their best then. As you went upstairs the scent of the ripening apples was lovely and we eagerly awaited the day when Dad sent one of us to fetch one down; we watched while he cut into it with his penknife and tasted it, then gave us all a slice to try and waited for our verdict. They were lovely.

I had only heard people talk about bananas; I couldn't remember what they looked or tasted like. They were slow to come in after the war and in short supply. News items appeared in the papers with photos of children tasting their first banana, and I couldn't wait to have one.

One day Mr Randall came into the street. He had a fruit and vegetable shop at Berkeley, three miles away, and came regularly with fresh produce in the boot of his car to sell to the local people. On this particular day he had bananas. Mam never bought from him, as she considered him to be too expensive.

'Mam, Mam!' I wailed, 'Mr Randall's got bananas!' I watched my friends eating some out in the street and my mouth was watering. 'Go and get some Mam, go and get some' I begged.

'He won't let me have any' she answered.

'But try Mam, try!'

She took her purse from the drawer, glanced in the mirror at her brown curls and gave them a quick pat, then marched out and across the street, humming a little tune while she did so. I watched from inside. My heart was in my mouth and my nose was pressed against the window pane as I waited. I saw Mam's lips moving and then I saw Mr. Randall's dour face as he shook his head. Mam walked back empty-handed. There were no bananas for me that day.

Dad was in the Home Guard, as he was too old to be called up for active service. He dressed up in his khaki uniform once a week and went off to train with other chaps. Because he was in the Home Guard we had a supply of red buckets at home which had to be kept full of water at all times, and a stirrup pump to go with them, but I don't think it would have been very efficient at putting out fires. A bomb dropped in a field nearby once and I traipsed there with Henry to gaze at the hole it had made and view the shrapnel around.

'What shall we do Mam if there's an air raid?' I asked her once.

'Oh, we'll all get in the cupboard under the stairs,' she replied.

The tiny cupboard housed the gas meter and there wasn't room for anything else, but if Mam said we could all get in there then we could. I thought maybe we would drink some magic potion like Alice and shrink as we walked into the cupboard. Luckily it was never put to the test.

At the bottom of the street was an archway formed where a road went over the top, and it was filled in at each end with sandbags. This was our makeshift shelter, but only once did Mam leave her home, and that was in the middle of the night when the bombs were raining down on Bristol. As we looked towards the city the whole sky was glowing red.

'Oh, our poor Ivy, our poor Ivy,' Mam moaned. Ivy, her sister, lived in Bristol and was indeed suffering. She had to leap on the first bus passing by, in her night clothes and with two small boys, so that it would take her away from the burning city.

'Come on, get yer coats on,' Mam shouted, 'Let's get down to that shelter.' So we all hurried down the street and went into the shelter for the first and only time ever. It was well padded inside with sandbags lining the walls, and there were wooden benches to sit on. It was a novelty to me sitting there in my nightclothes with my friends, but after an hour Mam gathered us up, long before the all-clear sounded, and announced we were all going back home. Sharpness was too small and insignificant for Hitler to bother with.

Clothing was rationed too. We had to save up our coupons when we needed anything new, especially for big items like coats or shoes. Towards the end of the war we were able to get parachute silk. This was lovely soft white material, but we had to unpick the panels of the silk, which was quite time-consuming. We made underwear from it; petticoats, slips or french knickers. There was also a fabric for which you didn't need coupons which was known as crash; it was a plain cream or white coarse fabric and we used it for cushion covers or chair backs and spent our time embroidering them.

There was a lot of making do. Clothes were made to last as long as possible, with a lot of patching and darning. Shirt collars would be turned when they frayed. This meant painstakingly unpicking the collar from the shirt and turning it and stitching it back on so that the frayed bit was underneath and couldn't be seen. Also shirts came with longer backs then, called tails, so there was plenty to tuck into trousers and it was possible to cut off the shirt tail and make a completely new collar out of it. Sheets were turned sides to middle when they became thin with wear. They were cut in half down the centre from top to bottom, then the sides were stitched together to make a new thicker middle. The raw outside edges were then hemmed to finish the job. Quite a lot of work, but it added life to the sheets and saved having to buy more.

Socks were always darned when holes appeared and stockings were repaired if they had a ladder. If a hole in a sock was very big I have known Mam to cut a patch from an old sock and stitch it on. Sometimes things had to be pulled back out of the rag bag, as it was better than what we were using. We wasted very little then. I remember, on very cold nights in winter, Mam putting a heavy army greatcoat on the bed to keep us warm because there were not enough blankets.

Each night Dad had to put up the blackout; thick black material nailed onto a wooden frame that fitted tightly against the window. Also the windows were covered with sticky tape criss-cross style, to stop the glass shattering if we were bombed. Dock police patrolled the area, and woe betide you if a chink of light was showing at the sides. 'Put that light out!' would be the cry. There were no street lamps and road signs were removed, so that the Germans would not know where they were if they invaded.

The grain silo, as it was so high, was camouflaged by painting it randomly in shades of khaki. We had German prisoners of war transported to Sharpness from Gloucester towards the end of the war. In groups of twenty or so they did menial tasks such as weeding the railway lines. They were well guarded and there was no problem.

For school, during the war, we had to cut out from the newspapers any news of the war with photos and maps showing the advance of our troops and about how the war was progressing, which we then stuck into a book. 'They printed that large enough' Mam said once and I looked at the front page of the *Daily Herald* to see 'COLOGNE OURS' in huge black letters filling up half of the page.

Our gas masks had to be carried with us at all times. The cardboard box containing your mask, or leather if you were lucky, was slung over your shoulders. The gasmask was horrid; black with rubber straps to go round your head. It was tight fitting, with a thing like a pig's snout. The end of the snout was metal with holes in and a filter to allow you to breathe, but the inside got very hot and wet and uncomfortable. We had to go on marches from school to practise wearing them in case of gas attacks near the school.

Evacuees came to stay at Sharpness during the war. Some from Bristol were very much like us country folk, and I made a lot of new friends. But a few from London were different. They looked delicate compared to us, as if a puff of wind would blow them away. One girl, Delphine Lee, arrived in my class one day and I looked at her in awe. Her hair was blonde, almost white and very fine; it framed a dainty face with skin like the palest porcelain and china blue eyes. She stood in my classroom wearing a pink silk pleated skirt and a shell pink fluffy angora jumper. Her shoes were black patent ankle straps and her socks were very white. Mam would never let me have black, patent ankle straps no matter how many times I begged.

I glanced at my sensible, brown lace-ups, grey socks, navy skirt and cardie and thought this girl was too good to be true. The family she was staying with danced attendance on her, wrapped her in a cocoon of protection and warned any rough locals not to touch her. A few children like that came to Sharpness and were viewed with curiosity.

It wasn't until the war was over that we read of the full horrors of Auschwitz and Belsen, or of our poor soldiers at Dunkirk. We were shown film on the Gaumont British News at the cinema of how the war was progressing, but it was always good news; advancing troops or anything to keep up morale. As VE day approached everyone was in buoyant mood. On that date I was sleeping at Auntie Sarah's. Her son, Cyril, my cousin, was a good footballer and he played for Bristol Rovers, so he was away from home at weekends. Auntie Sarah was nervous of sleeping alone in the house, so quite often I went along to keep her company. On that weekend she had said that I could take a friend, so Mary came with me. We slept in a big double bed, but we were woken up at midnight by a continuous hooting from all the ships and tugs that were in the dock. This rude awakening always happened to mark some important event, especially at twelve midnight at the start of every New Year. We lay for a while in the dark listening to the heralding sounds from all parts of the dock.

'I think the war is over,' I whispered. And we both went back to sleep.

Dad's grandparents and Uncle John outside the cottage at Berkeley Heath

Grammy Bennett in her feather boa with Grampy, sitting in front
of the ivy-covered wall of 12 Dinmore Road

Celebrating the Coronation of George VI on May 12 1937

Aerial view of Sharpness Dock, showing two piers, the basin and lock gates

A busy dockside scene

The old Severn Railway Bridge, demolished in the 1960s

Dad with Bridget and Julie with the pen in the background

Grandfather sitting on a wall

On the milk round with Darkie

On holiday at Weston Super Mare with Auntie Lil and Uncle Bert. Cousin Phyllis is in the centre, her daughter Marina on her left, and I am on the right

Henry on Julie outside
11 Bridge Road

On Julie at Berkeley Show

Mum and Dad in the garden of 11 Bridge Road, the street visible behind

SHOPPING

When Dad was a lad there was a shop by the Low Bridge, but when I was growing up it had been converted into two houses for the bridgemen and their families to live in. The shop, owned by Warren G. Smith, consisted of a tailors and outfitters, a hosiery and hatters, a drapery and a boot and shoe department, all in little Sharpness. There was plenty of business then in the thriving port.

I long to look into the windows in the picture to see what they were wearing in the early 1900s, but the photo I have of it has been copied so many times that the picture is a blur. I wonder what kind of underwear is in the drapery window; bodices, corsets and chemises? In the outfitting window there appears to be a row of top hats, all with white silk lining. I think they would also have sold thick jerseys for the sailors, and oilskins and sou'westers. And perhaps the handmade leather thigh boots in which the soles were fixed with wooden pegs which, when wet, would swell, making the boots watertight.

Mrs Tucker's shop was the one I went to with Mam. Her grocery shop was in Bridge Road, between the bridgemen's houses and the offices belonging to Mousell, Chadbourn and Taylor, a firm which supplied lighters to convey timber on the canal. When George Tucker was alive it would have been a very busy shop providing provisions to the many ships in the dock, but trade had slackened by the 1940s and Mrs Tucker ran the business single-handed.

A glazed door led into the shop and an enormous green bell clanged above our heads as we stepped inside to be met by an array of aromas; spices, cheese, bacon, all mixed with a hint of paraffin. At the one end of the shop, huge meathooks protruded from the ceiling where sides of meat and bacon used to hang, giving us a clue to its former glory. Mrs Tucker bustled in from the back room where she lived.

'A pound of bacon is it, Mrs Bennett?' Mrs Tucker asked, as with lightning moves she flashes the silver blade of her carving knife against the steel. 'Yes please and nice and thick, 'cos we're having it for dinner today' replied Mam. The butcher's block was thick, scrubbed white and scarred with a thousand cleavers.

As well as the bacon, the butter, cheese and lard had to be cut by hand and weighed. It sat in enormous slabs behind the counter. A morsel of cheese was offered on the point of a knife for tasting and Mam's approval. Butter was shaped into neat rectangles with wooden butter pats, then expertly wrapped in greaseproof paper. All the weighing was done on huge brass scales, balancing the goods with weights from the tiny half ounce up to a heavy, square ten-pounder. Mrs Tucker was very good at making bags from a square of paper. Holding one corner between her thumb and forefinger she flipped the paper expertly around her hand, then twisted the bottom and she had a perfect cone. After filling it with sweets or spices she tucked in the top flap and there was a neat little packet, just right for small hands.

Lined up on the back wall behind the counter were large green tins, about eight of them, in the shape of milk churns and nearly as big. They were a dull colour now; the once glistening gold writing of 'Tea', 'Sugar' and 'Currants' had dulled to a murky yellow ochre. Tins of biscuits sat fat and square on a shelf; I liked to read the names; Marie, Rich Tea, Osborne and Petit Beurre, all 1/2d per pound.

Mrs Tucker pulled out a handful of Rich Tea, slipped them into a paper bag and popped them on the scales. 'Can Henry come down after school, I've a few orders to go out?' she said. 'Yes,' Mam nodded, 'I'll send him down.' My brother used to deliver groceries to customers to earn some pocket money; he used a bicycle with a basket set into a metal frame on the front. Mam caught up with the local gossip and I gazed about.

The sweet jars, tiered on shelves, were just behind the door. There were row upon row of delectable colours and shapes; jelly babies, barley sugar twists, aniseed balls and liquorice comfits.

Mam's sister, Ivy, was in service in Clifton, Bristol, and sometimes brought things for me that were no longer wanted at the big house. One item was a toy dog. It was of white silky fur with one black ear and glass eyes. The head was hard stuffed, but the body was empty, with a zip along its back, as it was really a nightdress case. You put your nightclothes in it, then arranged it on the bed in a lying position. It was my constant companion to cuddle in bed for many years as I had never had a teddy bear or any soft toy.

Another thing she brought was a bag; like a clutch evening bag in a floral fabric. It was the fastener on the front that attracted me, as it looked just like a Smartie, except they weren't called Smarties then, probably they were known as chocolate beans. Anyway one day I decided I wanted some sweets that looked like that and couldn't remember what they were called, so I started to search for the bag; I was absolutely certain that if I could show Mam the kind of sweets I wanted she would let me have some. I searched high and low, but the bag was nowhere to be seen.

'Stop brevitting in that drawer my girl' Mam scolded.

'But Mam I'm looking for that bag Auntie Ivy gave me because the fastener is just like the sweets I want.'

I couldn't find it. I rather think Mam had had one of her clear outs; she was apt to do that kind of thing. I never saw the bag again and I never got any sweets that day either.

Mrs Tucker often gave me dummy chocolate bars from her window display. These were usually made of wood or cardboard and were lovely for playing shops, but one, a tin for Fry's chocolate cream, looked so real with its coating of dark, glistening paint that it was a job not to take a bite of it. When she packed up and left in 1942 she gave me a paper sunshade, pleated and decorated with bright flowers and ladies in kimonos. I felt very elegant whenever I used it.

Albert Sumption was a veteran of the First World War and his shop was just across the Low Bridge on a grassy patch. It was a single storey, all made of wood. Many years before there had been a three-storeyed lodging house and tearooms on the site, also made of wood, for men to stay the night when they came looking for work at Sharpness. They used to walk from Gloucester along the canal bank and were issued with a token which allowed them to stay for the night. When the lodging house was demolished Albert Sumption built his shop there and carried on the tearooms with a grocery business as well.

Albert was a slight chap with thinning grey hair and a limp. He had lost a leg during the war and it was replaced with a wooden one which made a loud thump as he moved about the wooden floors. He was also slightly deaf and always leaned over the counter towards me with his hand cupped around his ear to hear what a small girl had to say. At bait and dinner times the dockers poured into his little tearoom to enjoy Albert's tea and sandwiches. 'A cup o' tea and a cheese sandwich please Albert' they would say. When he had a customer in the shop as well he got a bit agitated and had a nervous cough. 'Be with you in a minute,' he called as he stumped about carrying trays of hot tea to the grateful dockers.

Albert lived at Newtown, but he always walked the mile to his shop and back again at night in spite of having a wooden leg. 'There goes Albert,' Mam would say as he passed our house. Like all shops during the war there were many empty shelves, but I enjoyed going in to spend my sweet coupons.

When the war was over a Lyons van began to call at the shop once a week on Thursdays to deliver cakes. What a treat. 'Mam, Lyons van has just gone over the bridge, can I go and get a cake?' I shouted. 'Wait a minute then, give them time to unload.' Then I sped over the bridge to get our ration. You were never allowed more than one. Sometimes it was a few currant buns, or a Swiss roll, or a French jam sandwich, looking every bit as good as it did on the box; a light fluffy sponge with a layer of cream and thick strawberry jam. But my favourite was a Snow Cake, a round sponge cake topped with thick marshmallow and sprinkled with coconut. Lovely.

Dock Row boasted a chemist and a Post Office and the docks canteen was nearby. At this end, adjacent to the lock gates, was a row of shops built of wood. Mr Conway was a cobbler by trade and sold shoes as well. The pungent aroma of leather, dyes, glue and polishes met you as you stepped into the tiny shop and also the sounds of whirring machinery or the banging of nails into leather.

Mr Conway was a pleasant chap, always ready to pass the time of day chatting of times gone by; he was full of interesting anecdotes. He would bustle out from his workroom into the little shop, short and dumpy and wrapped in his leather apron, a few grey curls on his balding head, slightly protruding eyes and a goitre swelling in his throat, he looked every inch a cobbler. 'Yes, she went down with all hands lost, tragic it was, en route from New York to Shanghai, never seen again' he would say. He was always full of stories about sailors and the sea.

Gwillum Evans ran the newsagents next door. He delivered the papers all over the docks. We had the *Daily Herald*, a serious broadsheet newspaper. It wasn't until I went out to work that I discovered that there were more frivolous types of papers such as *Reveille* and *Titbits*. Mam wouldn't have them in the house. I was allowed the *Girl's Crystal* or *School Friend*, papers with schoolgirl stories in, but never anything like *Sunny Stories* by Enid Blyton. Luckily I had a friend, Wendy, whose mother bought her *Sunny Stories,* and every so often she gave me a bundle and I crept into a corner and lost myself in the imaginings of Enid Blyton. Wendy's mother let her have black patent anklestrap shoes too. I always admired them and the way they clattered as she walked.

I went to this shop for Dad's ounce of A1 tobacco and green cigarette papers and Gwillum Evans always peered over the top of his spectacles as I went in. I loved to look in the window at the books, fountain pens and other stationery. Inside the whole of the back wall was taken up with rows of books and served as the local library. As with other shops Evans' would have seen better days.

Vessels known as steam packets were based at Gloucester and made regular trips along the canal to Sharpness, bringing lots of visitors with them. On the way they stopped off at Quedgeley,

Slimbridge, The Patch and Framilode. *The Wave* and *Lapwing* were immaculately kept, with decks scrubbed white. In summer they were decorated with red, white and blue flags and sported large white awnings for shade. Sharpness people used them to go to Gloucester for their shopping and goods were transported on them.

I have a pink lustre jug with 'A Present from Sharpness' on it in gold writing and printed on the base is 'Made in Germany'. I bought in in the 1960s from a second-hand shop in Gloucester and I think it came from Evans' in those days of prosperity when visitors liked to take a present home.

The Pier Refreshment Rooms was the name of the next shop. It was owned by Mr Davis, who had been a captain in the Royal Navy, and with his stern bulldog face he looked the part and I was scared of him. In its heyday all the visitors to the docks would have poured in for their refreshments and it would have been very different from the shop I knew. Part of the shop was still used as a tearoom by the dockers; it was full of long wooden tables and benches.

During the war the shop window had nothing in it, just empty wooden shelves. They wouldn't have had many sweets anyway, but I was in with a chance because my cousin Anita went to school with the daughter of the establishment, Kathleen. If we called in to spend our sweet ration, 4oz each month, a box or two of sweets were drawn out furtively from under the counter, chewing nuts, marzipan teacakes or jelly beans, and I watched eagerly as Kathleen weighed out two ounces and put them in a paper bag. We wandered back along the dockside on our Sunday afternoon walk to see what ships were in and now and then dipped our hands into our pockets to reach for another sweet to pop in our mouths.

Gassers, next to Davis's, was another ship's stores and grocery shop. Mrs Gasser served in the shop while Mr Gasser looked after the ships' provisions. His father had started the business, but the present Mr Gasser seemed old to me when I was young; he often stood in the doorway of his shop in his white overall and rubbed his hands, whistling under his breath and nodding his pink bald head. They still had a good grocery business with lads on bicycles delivering the goods.

Last of all in the line-up was a ship's chandlers, Johns and Sons, who also had a business in Commercial Road in Gloucester. Everything necessary for a busy port was sold there; stout rope, heavy coils of chain, canvas, awnings and tarred marline. The smell of tarred marline stayed with me forever.

RELATIONS

Dad was the youngest of ten children, so I always had plenty of aunties, uncles, cousins and second cousins around me. Apart from Uncle Harry, one of Dad's older brothers who emigrated to America in 1910, all the others stayed in Gloucestershire.

My grandparents, Henry and Emma Bennett, moved into a house at the bottom of the street, 12 Dinmore Road, when the houses were built. Dad was born there in 1902. My grandfather was a dock policeman so their house, on the end of the row, was slightly better than those in the terrace with an open outlook from the extra side windows and a much bigger garden. The garden was big enough for vegetables and there was still room for a lawn with a seat under a trellis arch which, every summer, was festooned with red and cream roses.

In the photograph Grampy is sitting on a low wall made of soft sandstone, it was rough and grainy; slightly orange in colour. It must have been ideal for sharpening pen knives, because all along the front edge were small indentations as smooth as marble and I could never resist running a finger along them, feeling the silky smoothness.

Although Grampy was on the photograph in 1937, when I was three, he must have died soon afterwards, because I can't remember much about him. I'm sure I would have been a bit scared of him, as he looks stern and has a large droopy moustache. He worked on the Low Bridge at one time, opening and closing it for the river traffic. There was an incident once when one ship passing through caused some damage to another and because of insurance it was taken to court and Grandfather had to travel to London as a witness. While giving his account of the incident he waved his arms about, explaining how it happened, and he sent a glass of water, which had been on the desk in front of him, flying across the room. The judge said, 'Witness A, it is all right to show how it was done, but don't hit things around.' Apparently the court erupted into laughter. While in London he went to a show with dancing girls and thoroughly enjoyed himself.

I never saw my grandmother walking, as she had had a stroke before I came on the scene and in those days they didn't bother to exercise patients to try and recover some of their mobility but just left them to sit all day. Grammy always sat in a chair near the window where she could see people pass by on the high road above the house.

When I was small I was often lifted up and placed on her lap. I sat very still and didn't dare move but gazed at her smooth round face and white hands, noticing her nails, which I always thought looked like blanched almonds. She smelled of freshly-laundered linen. She had short legs so she had a very little lap, but she was plump and well-padded. Auntie Lil lived with her and she and Auntie Dor, who lived in the street too, saw to all of her needs, getting her up in the morning and putting her to bed at night.

Harry, who had gone to America, had written a journal of his life and from that I had a little insight of what Grammy had been like in her younger days. She was a keen churchgoer and an active member of the community, always helping at special times like Sunday school tea parties. When Harry brought his young wife, Nellie, back to Sharpness to visit, one of the outings she arranged was to hire a pony and trap and take them to Shepperdine for a ride, just as Henry and I did twenty-five years later.

She lost a son, Jesse, in the First world War. He died in France in 1918 and is buried there. She used to meet up with other mothers who had lost sons and they talked together and gave each other support. Grammy had a breakdown when she had the news and never really recovered from it; she became forgetful and tearful, always talking of her boy who 'should never have gone to war'.

When I was about eight years old I went with Mam to Auntie Lil's house and she led us into the front room, where there was a huge box supported on chairs. It was too high for me to see what was inside, but Mam and Auntie Lil peered in and talked in hushed tones.

'Shall I pick her up to see?' Auntie Lil asked Mam. Mam nodded and I was lifted up and looked into the coffin and there was Grammy, waxen and peaceful, her almond hands crossed over her breast forever.

Auntie Lil and Uncle Bert stayed on at 12 Dinmore Road. Auntie Lil was prim and proper, with coarse grey hair severely combed back and finished with a roll of curls around her neck. Uncle Bert operated the low swing bridge. They had never had any children of their own but were always willing to look after other people's children, so Mam often left me with Auntie Lil while she went shopping. I always went willingly; they were good and kind and enjoyed having me.

When I was almost nine years of age, Mam said I had to go and sleep at Auntie Lil's for a few nights and Henry was to come too, but he only stayed one night and he was off home refusing to stay any more. When we awoke the next morning Auntie Lil broke the news to us that we had a baby brother. We larked and giggled as we went up the street after breakfast, excited at seeing the new baby. He was a bruiser of a baby and his name was Ronald Jeffrey.

My life changed after that, because I was expected to help Mam more in the house. I hated standing in the garden rocking the pram until the baby went to sleep; I wanted to be out playing with my friends. And, of course, my nose was pushed out; until then I had been the baby of the family.

As my father was the youngest of ten children, by the time he was born the older siblings had moved out into homes of their own and were having babies themselves. But it must have been exciting for them moving to 12 Dinmore Road, because they had moved from a cottage that had no gas or electricity. These houses has gas laid on, as the gasometer was not far away. They had a gas stove for cooking and gas lights. These were gas mantles that hung from the ceiling and were made of white gauze, small and round, the size of an eggcup. The gas would be turned on and it made a satisfying pop as a match was put to the mantle. Then it hissed away as it was burning and made another plop as it was turned out. Electricity was still some years off.

Before this they had lived in cottages without even running water. Now they could light their house with gas and cook by it too, instead of relying on an open fire. Candles still had to be used in the bedrooms, and with only three bedrooms there was plenty of sharing. The girls were allocated the front bedroom and the boys the tiny back bedroom at the end of a passage. As only one candle was allowed when they went to bed, it was placed halfway along the passage to serve both rooms, but the girls would creep out of bed and gleefully pull it nearer to their door and then the boys would creep out and pull it back again. And so it went on, with much arguing on both sides.

The houses were built in 1879, so there had been a community there many years before my time and I loved hearing about the old times.

For years there was a huge jigsaw puzzle at Auntie Lil's, set out on the table in the front room. It was of the liner *Queen Mary* with lots of sea and sky, and was in the process of being completed. Anyone visiting would wander in and try and fit in a piece or two and emerge with satisfaction if they succeeded.

Sometimes I went for an evening to play a game of cards. We all sat around the dining table and played Market, where you had to end up with a set of the same animal on your cards. You could swop as many as you liked at one go, so there were shouts of, 'One one one!' or 'Three three three!' waving our cards madly in the air for takers, then moans if the swopped ones weren't of the set we were collecting or glee if they were. Eventually someone called 'Market!' having a full set, and that was it for that game.

We had some good parties there with old-fashioned games. For one we had to go out of the room while someone was dressed in an old coat and sat in a chair. One player was blindfolded and led in and was made to feel the person in the chair. Then Auntie Lil said, 'Now you know about Nelson who fought at Trafalgar and how he lost a leg? Well this is where his leg should have been,' and our hand was directed at an empty trouser leg. After a feel of the empty trouser leg and an agreement that there was no leg there, Auntie Lil continued, 'He lost an arm too, you feel his empty sleeve,' so we did and agreed there was no arm. 'He lost an eye too,' Auntie Lil continued and at that we squealed and pulled away. 'Well, you feel his eye,' she would say, and your hand was firmly grasped and a finger gouged into… not an eye of course, but half an orange. The tension built up as the others waiting their turn outside the door listened to the screams.

After the war Auntie Lil and Uncle Bert took me on holiday

with them to Weston Super Mare. Mam and Dad had never wanted to go away and I had only been for the day on the Sunday School treat, so seven days staying in a guest house, with lots of ice creams, candyfloss, peppermint rock, sea and sand was lovely to me. My cousin Phyllis and her daughter Marina came too. Marina was the same age as me; she was pretty and dainty. The men staying at the guest house liked to talk to her and one always called her 'his little fairy' when we went into the dining room.

One day Marina tied her silk square around her neck as we were getting ready to go out. I didn't have one. 'Would you like to borrow mine?' Auntie Lil offered. So I did; it was burnished gold and amber silk, which seemed to change colour as you looked at it in a different light. It was edged with a silky fringe.

Mam made all my clothes; she was a good dressmaker and she enjoyed sewing. Not just dresses and blouses but shorts and jackets too. Every day on holiday at Weston we went to the same ice cream parlour near the beach where we had ice cream cones, the tops of which had been dipped into melted chocolate. By the time we started to eat them the chocolate had set solid and cracked as we bit into it.

We had to stay outside until our evening meal and one day we couldn't decide what to do as it was a dull, windy day. The sand blew up in our faces so we ensconced ourselves on the beach, having hired windbreaks as well as deckchairs. The windbreaks were erected in a ring all around us and we sat there with our books and magazines while the wind howled. I thought it was fun and an adventure in our little shelter.

MAM'S FAMILY

My maternal grandfather, Caleb Skidmore, played the music to accompany silent films. He was a good violinist, a gift he had inherited from his father. He teamed up with a Mr Summers who played the piano, and together they made a good pair. My grandfather arranged all the music to suit which films were being shown; lively for the cowboys on galloping horses, sad and melancholy for tragedy and soft and romantic for the love scenes. They sat behind a screen to play, hidden from the audience but able to see the film and match the music to suit the films as the story progressed. Sometimes Lollie Lightfoot, a local girl, played the piano for him; she had a liking for Nuttall's Mintoes and he always had to bribe her with a bagful. She put them on the piano to enjoy throughout the evening.

They were much in demand for their music, not only at the local parish room where the films were put on but around many villages in Gloucestershire; Wotton, Cam, Dursley and Berkeley.

He was well known in the area. They also played music for the local dances; these too were held in the parish room, where many of the men from boats in the dock at the time enjoyed an evening dancing with the local girls. Grandmother provided the refreshments and made a nice little profit for her hard work.

Grandfather invited musicians from the ships to his home for a musical evening. They came with a variety of instruments, having come from foreign parts; mandolins with colourful streamers fluttering from them, harmonicas, penny whistles and balalaikas. Grandmother put on a simple spread - slices of meat from the weekend joint, hunks of bread and pickled onions and piccalilli - and everyone had a good time.

Grandfather gave violin lessons in the front room, where a fire had been lit to warm it in readiness for the learners. Not many people could afford lessons, but he always had a few practising *The Blue Bells of Scotland* or *The Rose of Tralee*. He was a lovely man, quiet and gentle and very clever with his hands. He made the first wireless in the area, and many people reminded me of it. He worked from a diagram, not only assembling the parts but making the components as well, such as coils of spring steel.

He had taken his young family to Wales, near Abergavenny, to find employment when there was not enough work at Sharpness and Mam was born there. As trade increased on the docks he came back to live on the New Road at Newtown. He died from lung cancer when I was quite young. I wish I had known him better and had been able to listen to his violin playing.

When he died a daughter of a neighbour was sent to tell Mam. There weren't many telephones then; people couldn't afford them. Mam answered the door to the knock and the girl told her the sad news of her father's death and Mam thanked her and closed the door, then leaned her head against the doorpost and sobbed loudly. 'Don't cry Mam, don't cry,' I said, tugging at her sleeve. I couldn't bear to see my mother cry.

Mam remembered going to see her grandmother; she lived in a thatched cottage hidden in the fold of a field behind the New Road. You couldn't see the cottage until you were almost upon it. She was often sent to stay with her and she loved it. Her grandmother would sit down in front of the fire with her and read a book to her, or take an old sock and fashion it into a doll with her needle and thread with buttons for eyes and hair in long woollen plaits. A big sepia photograph of her grandmother hung on our landing for years. I thought she looked stern in her high-necked dress, but they never smiled for the camera back then. I always enjoyed Mam's stories about her.

Auntie Ivy was Mam's sister, but they were as different as chalk and cheese. Mam was serious, a quiet and private person. Auntie Ivy was talkative, full of fun and always laughing. Her blue eyes twinkled and her head would go back and merry sounds erupted from her. No one was miserable when Auntie Ivy was around.

When I was little I often noticed a secret smile playing around Mam's lips as she carried out her daily chores. I wanted to share it too and said, 'Mam what are you smiling about?' She replied with a toss of her head, 'I'm not smiling, it's just my normal happy disposition.' But I knew different; she had a secret which she wouldn't share with me.

At school Mam was always held up as a shining example to poor Auntie Ivy. She was two years younger than Mam and the teachers would chide her. 'Why aren't you more like your sister Winnie?' they said whenever she was in trouble at school, which was often, as she liked to play truant. 'The sun shone out of her bottom as far as those teachers were concerned,' laughed Ivy telling me all about it in later years, so she hated her when they were growing up.

When Auntie Ivy went home from school for lunch, she always had to walk over to the dock where her father worked with his dinner or 'bait'. She told me in later years how she stopped under the railway bridge she had to cross to reach the docks and opened up the dinner and ate some of the sandwich filling, or took the cloth off the cooked meal in the chipped, brown enamel basin and ate the top of it. When her father got home that night he would complain, saying, 'That was a measly dinner you sent over today, Missus.'

When Mam and Dad were courting they used to walk to the old dock, where it was quiet and secluded. This was really out of bounds, as her parents had told her not to go there. Ivy knew this, so when Mam got home and they were in bed together Ivy always demanded the chocolate dragees that Dad had bought for her. 'If you don't give me those chocolates I'll tell where you've been,' she threatened.

Mam was always a gardener and liked to grow flowers at home, forget-me-nots and cornflowers. She had her own bit of garden, but Auntie Ivy would come along and stamp on them and kick the soil around to get her own back. All this sibling rivalry sorted itself out when they grew up.

When Auntie Ivy was fourteen she left school and went into service, as many young girls did in those days. It was arranged for her to go to a place at Filton in Bristol, so with trepidation and her trunk packed with all her worldly possessions she waited for the bus to Bristol outside the Pier View Hotel at Newtown. The bus driver had been instructed where to put her off at Gloucester Road in Filton, and when the destination was reached she was set down outside some big, iron gates leading up to the big house. She made her way with her trunk to the front door and rang the bell and was admitted into the kitchen. Her first job was to make tea for the family: the children of the house sniggered and made fun of her as they peeped around the door to see what the new 'skivvy' looked like.

On the first day she was in the kitchen alone when a hatch slid open and a plate was pushed through; on it was just a boiled rabbit's head covered with sauce. That was all. It was her dinner and her introduction to working in service. She had never had to eat rabbit's head before; rabbits were plentiful in the country.

Her bedroom was at the top of the house in one of the attics, and one night she was so unhappy that she sat up into the night by the light of a candle stub, writing a heartfelt letter to her sister Phyllis, who was four years older and also in service at Bristol.

She begged her to come and take her away from the place. As she was writing, the door flew open and an apparition in white stood there. It was the woman of the house in a voluminous white nightgown; she had seen the light under the door and demanded to know what she was doing wasting a candle well into the night. The woman blew out the candle and told her to get to bed, but not before she had confiscated the 'Snowfire' hand cream Ivy had been about to rub on her poor chapped hands. The grease would get on the sheets, the woman had told her. Auntie Ivy didn't stay long at that place.

She was often getting into trouble breaking the crockery. At one place where she worked they had a long dresser full of china; complete dinner and tea services which were used every day. The name of the design was Indian Tree; it was green and pink with gold rims. Whenever she broke a piece she was sent post-haste to the shop to get a replacement to keep the service complete. This happened so often that the name of the china was etched in her memory for evermore.

Years later, when she was in her eighties, I went with her to a fete where they had a bric-a-brac stall and she saw a plate that was familiar to her. 'That's Indian Tree,' she said to the stallholder, who picked up the plate and examined the back. 'You're right, it is,' she said. I bought the plate for her and it now hangs on her dining room wall as a memento of hard times.

The work was hard, but it was good training for when they had their own homes to run. They were among the gentry and the high standard of living rubbed off on them. They were taught to do things well, and that teaching never left them. Many's the time Mam has scorned me for not carrying out some task properly, such as scraping carrots. 'You don't do it like that, you do it like this,' she said, taking the carrot off me and proceeding to scrape it away from her into the sink instead of towards her as I had been doing. The way they were taught was the correct way and they could see no other.

Auntie Ivy met her husband, Doug, in Bristol and they settled down there and had two sons. After the war, when they had been rehoused, I was invited to go and stay with them and I always enjoyed it. I always loved Auntie Ivy; she was such fun, laughed a lot and was always interested in what I had been up to. 'Joyce,' she would say, 'Come and sit by me and tell me what you have been doing.' I always loved that, it was a novelty for me. I caught the bus outside the Pier View Hotel, travelled to the centre of Bristol and then got a bus to Brislington. Auntie Ivy had told me where to get off and it was just a short walk to Sherwell Road where they lived. As I was only about twelve at the time it seemed like a big adventure to me.

Everything was so different from life at home. There was a bathroom upstairs; a room with a white bath, a toilet and a basin too. The water gushed out of the taps, sparkling and clean. There was no zinc bath to be unhooked from an outside nail and carried in to be filled. If the tap was left running for a moment or the potatoes were peeled under running water I couldn't get over the waste; I was used to saving water because it all had to be carried in from the pump. And Auntie's washing looked so fresh and white. No smuts from passing engines or dust from ship's cargoes here.

The food tasted better as well. Auntie Ivy made lovely chunky potato chips and sometimes I had date sandwiches for breakfast, which I enjoyed. The bread tasted different, the water tasted different, everything was different.

'Look Doug, doesn't Joyce look nice in her curlers?' Auntie Ivy said one night when I was ready for bed and we were settling down together and tuned into the Home Service on the wireless to listen to a play. Mam wouldn't have said that, she would think I was getting above my station.

During my stay in Bristol we did lots of different things and always together as a family. They took me to the cinema to see *In Which we Serve* or *The Way to the Stars*, with John Mills and Michael Redgrave. Or to the Speedway once, which was new to me. The revving of the motorbikes started each race and round they would come, engines roaring louder and louder as they approached, so near you could feel the heat of them. Once they were past, the smell of exhaust got up your nose, as well as bits of the cinder track which flew up as they rounded the corners and stuck to your face and clothes. Then there was the excitement of waiting for the next race to begin.

Another outing we went on was to Brandon Hill, just Auntie Ivy and us children as Uncle Doug was at work. We children went off enjoying ourselves on the swings, leaving Auntie Ivy sitting under a tree. But we hadn't been there long when she called out that we must go. She gathered us up and hurried us on, saying she didn't like the look of a man nearby. I was sorry to leave as we had only just got there and were having a good time. It wasn't until I was grown up that she explained that the man had exposed himself to her. No wonder she wanted to get away.

We visited the Cabot Tower. John Cabot was an explorer who settled in Bristol and the tower is a memorial to him. It was very high with a spiral staircase inside to climb to the top. 'Now, it's a bit narrow Joyce, especially as you get to the top,' Auntie Ivy told me. 'But it's all right as long as you don't meet a fat person on their way down.' We laughed and made our way up and were nearly at the top, negotiating the narrowest bit of all when a rather rotund gentleman was advancing towards us. 'Oh, dear,' I heard Auntie Ivy groan, as she herself was not very sylph-like, but she was soon giggling as they struggled past one another tummy to tummy. The view over Bristol was worth the climb.

I loved going to stay with Auntie Ivy.

A VISIT TO HOSPITAL

There was only one time in my childhood that I remember with dread, and even today I can't bear to bring it to mind.

I was about eight at the time and Mam never warned me that anything unpleasant was about to happen that day, but I suppose she wouldn't have as she would have thought 'ignorance is bliss'. She just said we had an appointment, but didn't tell me where.

We caught the bus to Berkeley. 'We're a bit early, we'll go for a walk down by the castle' Mam said. I held her hand as we walked and looked at the huge walls of Berkeley Castle and over the castle meadows, but I began to feel a bit apprehensive as this wasn't the normal thing to do. Eventually we made our way back into Berkeley town and I was standing with Mam outside a door. In response to her ring on the bell I heard footsteps crossing the stone floor and a woman, all in starchy white, opened the door to us. I looked up at her face. On her head was a crisp, white square of fabric knotted at the nape which stuck out each side of her face.

Mam murmured something to her and I was gently pushed inside. And then, slam! The great, heavy door was shut, leaving my mother on the outside and me inside. I was scared then; I couldn't believe Mam would leave me like that. The starchy nurse took me to a small room and made me undress, then put me into a shapeless gown, long and white, which tied at the back. She dragged out a cardboard box from under a table. It was full of rubber caps, like shower caps but made of thick red rubber with elastic all around the edge. She sorted through them for size and tried one or two on my head, pulling my hair in the process, then decided on one and tugged it on me, pushing all my hair up inside as she did so. It was tight and uncomfortable and the elastic bit into my forehead.

She then led me to another room which was brightly lit. The walls were lined with children sitting on hard wooden chairs and they, like me, were wearing long white gowns and tight rubber caps. I was ushered to a chair against the wall and left.

We all sat in stunned silence, no one daring to move, no one knowing where to look. We waited and waited for what seemed forever to a small child. The elastic of the cap dug into my tender skin and hurt and itched; I longed to rub it away, but I was too scared to move. If I moved, all those eyes would turn towards me, so I sat very still and tried to forget the pain and the itching. Not knowing where to look, I focused my eyes on a black spot on the door. Keep on looking at the spot, I thought, and something will happen.

Eventually the nurse appeared again and called a name and the child who answered to it was taken away to the mysterious unknown. The rest of us went on waiting until the nurse came back and took away another child.

At last she came for me. She took my hand and led me along a corridor, like a lamb to the slaughter. We came to a small room which was very brightly lit and inside was a man in white with a kind of torch thing strapped around his head. There was a high, narrow bed in the room against the wall. 'Climb up,' he ordered and I did. When I was lying down I looked up to see a piece of white gauze lowered over my face, 'Count to ten,' the voice snapped, and I began. One, two, three, four, five....

And so my tonsils and adenoids were removed, and a right mess they made of it, according to doctors who have peered down my throat since. I awoke in the night to the sound of a boy vomiting in the next bed. We were on low camp beds set very close together, rows and rows of them. I drifted back to sleep and was woken by a nurse offering me a drink of water from a teapot-shaped thing. My throat hurt, but the tight rubber cap was gone.

In the morning Mam was there to dress me and take me home. She had teamed up with another mother whose child had had their tonsils out and they shared the cost of a taxi between them. I was put straight to bed at home and Auntie Lil came into the room.

'Here Winnie,' she said, 'I've just baked her a lovely egg custard, it'll slip down a treat.' Dear Auntie Lil.

But maybe I was lucky, because in *Boy*, Roald Dahl's autobiography of his childhood, he tells the tale of having his adenoids out without anaesthetic; just sitting in a chair like you would at the dentist. And then walking the mile home. This happened in Norway in 1924. Although Dahl declares it to be true, he was such a great storyteller that I'm not sure I believe him.

Mr and Mrs Peglar, who lived at the bottom of the street, had two dogs; one was a terrier and the other a liver and white springer spaniel. Once I was down by the Low Bridge when Mr Peglar came along with his dogs and as he stopped I bent over to say hello to the springer spaniel and patted him on the head. I may have startled him, because he snapped at me and caught the corner of my lip between his teeth. Blood spurted out.

Mam looked at the wound and decided that I needed to see the doctor, so one was called. Dr Briers, from Berkeley, came and was admitted through the front door into the best room and while I stood there he stitched up my lip. It hurt a lot as the thin wire was pushed through my flesh, but I put up with it without a word. Every time I smiled it pulled on the wound, so I told everyone not to say anything to make me smile. I was scared when the time came to have the stitches out. I didn't feel a thing, but I bear the scar to this day.

There were many diseases to be feared when I was a child. Diphtheria and smallpox could be prevented by the use of vaccinations, but these cost money, so many poorer children died from them. The National Health Service and its free treatment didn't begin until after the war, when the Labour Government won the election with Clement Attlee at the helm. Poliomyelitis was greatly feared, as there was no vaccine for it. It was thought to be spread by flies, so all food was kept covered or stored in a safe or larder. Children with polio became paralysed and spent long periods in hospital, sometimes needing to be put in an iron lung to help with their breathing. Even if they recovered, many were paralysed for life.

There was no prevention for other childhood diseases such as measles, mumps, chickenpox or whooping cough. We suffered from them all as a matter of course and generally came out unscathed. Scarlet fever was more serious and the patient had to be isolated to stop the disease spreading, so isolation hospitals were set up.

There was no immunisation from tuberculosis either. Patients were sent to hospital for long periods and often had their beds outside in the fresh air to aid recovery. When I worked on a farm delivering milk, 'tuberculin tested' milk was brought in as it was thought that milk from cows with the disease could pass it on to humans, so all cows had to be tested for TB and any found with the disease were destroyed.

Penicillin, the forerunner of antibiotics, was discovered by Sir Alexander Fleming during the war and used to treat wounded soldiers. Many more antibiotics are now available and many fatal illnesses have been prevented.

Mam had a younger brother named Raymond. When he was about three years old he fell and cut his leg when toddling in the garden. The cut turned septic and septicaemia set in and he died. Such a simple happening, but nothing could be done for him. That's the way it was then.

CHAPTER FOURTEEN

HIGH DAYS & HOLIDAYS

Compared to today, special occasions like Easter and Christmas were always low-key, but that didn't mean I didn't enjoy them as much; I hadn't known any different. Perhaps the one time we excelled was on Good Friday, when we eagerly awaited our hot cross buns. Our bread was delivered to the door then and always by Mr Sturge. He had a bakery in Newtown and the windows used to be whitewashed over to stop nosey children from staring in as he was preparing the dough. But on my way home from school I often looked for a spyhole and peered in to watch him working inside. He was a pleasant chap with grizzled hair and a rosy face and he always wore a sand-coloured coat overall and dark brown leather gaiters, tight and shiny around his legs.

It was the Sturges who owned the Plantation at one time and let out the grounds for parties. When they moved to Newtown Mrs Sturge opened a grocery shop next door to the bakery. Mam sent me for some fresh yeast once as she wanted to make some bread, but instead of asking for an ounce as I should have done, I asked for a pound. Mrs Sturge was taken aback and asked me if I was sure Mam had asked for a pound of yeast and perhaps it was an ounce, to which I agreed. She laughed and said, 'I thought your mother was going to make bread for the whole street.'

Mr Sturge came in a van and even on Good Friday we had our buns delivered to the door. He always came very early, while Mam and Dad were still in bed, so he must have been up all night to get all the buns ready as they were still warm when he brought them. Henry and I were up early in anticipation and kept running down to see if they were there.

At last we went to the doorstep and there were four paper bags, each bag containing four buns. We grabbed them and dashed back to Mam and Dad's bedroom and sat on the end of the bed while Mam and Dad sat up and we all enjoyed munching our buns. They were warm, yellow, sweet and dotted with currants. Four each! What greedy pigs we were!

I think the bun episode must have been before the war, because for months as Christmas approached, when food was rationed, Mam squirrelled away dried fruit, brown sugar and icing sugar in the pantry in readiness for a cake and puddings. She always added some gravy browning to the mixture to make the cake look darker and richer. The almond paste was padded out with semolina and flavoured with extra almond essence, as ground almonds were difficult to get. Sweet rations, too, were saved for Christmas so that we could have a few extra.

As Christmas drew near I knew there would be some sweets stashed away somewhere and I did my best to find them. When Mam was not around I went on a hunt; sometimes I was lucky, sometimes not. One year I looked behind a chest of drawers and saw a paper bag, so I pulled it out and it was full of Sharp's toffees. After helping myself to one I carefully put the bag back again. Mam never knew.

We always had one of our home-grown cockerels for Christmas dinner; it was a treat as we only had chicken once a year. There were no crackers or paper hats. Decorations were at a minimum, with a few home-made paper chains or some made from newspaper to string around the room. I don't remember a Christmas tree, but we sometimes brought in evergreens and hung little ornaments on them or blobs of cotton wool to look like snow. Presents were wrapped in brown paper and tied with string which had been saved up all the year.

I think I was too young when the war started to remember much about previous Christmases, except one, and that was when I started school. Only the infants had a present from Father Christmas, although everyone had a party tea. We had to take our own cup, dish and spoon, each clearly marked with our name stuck on underneath. After tea we went into the infants' classroom, where the dividing partition had been pushed back to make one big room. There was a magnificent Christmas tree, all decorated with presents and a Father Christmas to give them out. Each child had been asked what they wanted Father Christmas to bring them and I had said a tea set. 'Oh,' said Mam when I told her, 'you won't get that.' But I did; a china tea set, small but perfect; white with little red roses on. Such excitement, and never forgotten.

We always had a Sunday school tea party, but we had to go to Sunday school all the year to qualify. Dressed in our best clothes and on our best behaviour, we sat at long tables covered with snowy white cloths and had the usual jelly and ice cream, sandwiches and little fairy cakes, all washed down with a mug of orange squash. The tables were cleared away and we played games or sang songs while someone played the piano. At going-home time we lined up at the door and were given an orange and a present to take home.

Dad was like a child at Christmas. He always looked forward to it and talked about Father Christmas coming down the chimney (which, by the way, he had swept in readiness) and what he would bring us. But Mam said, 'Shush Alb, shush.' She didn't like us to get too excited and always played it down. She probably thought we would never get to sleep.

Of course we were excited as we climbed the stairs on Christmas Eve and hung our stockings on the bedpost. Several times I scrabbled down to the bottom of the bed to see if Father Christmas had been, and it was agony trying to get back to sleep. But eventually, usually about 2 am, I felt for the stocking and it was all hard and knobbly. I trembled with excitement as I unhooked it from the bedpost and scrambled back into bed. We had no light or heating in the bedroom, so all the opening of the stocking had to be done in the dark. There was always an orange in the toe and a few nuts in a paper bag; still in their shells, a sugar mouse and, perhaps a rolled up comic or a magic painting book that just needed a brush and water.

One year there was something hard and round, like a tin. 'I've got a tin of sweets,' I said to Henry. But try as I might, I couldn't open it. It felt as if it had a lid on top, but it just would not budge. I turned my attention to the base, rattling it to convince myself that it really was full of sweets. There was definitely something on the bottom and perhaps that was the way in, so my fingers picked and prised at it frantically at the thought of having a sweet. But it was no good, I just couldn't get into the thing. I gave up.

In the daylight next morning all was revealed; I had been struggling to open a moneybox in the shape of a round, red letterbox. The flap at the base, which had a keyhole in it and a tiny key to open it to get the money out, was broken beyond repair. Dad fixed it shut with a nut and bolt from Henry's Meccano, but it was never the same. I would rather have had a tin of sweets.

I usually had a new doll at Christmas, carefully dressed by Mam, and a book: Henry had Meccano or a Hornby Train set. As I grew older I had a fountain pen for school, a diary to write all my secrets in and Evening in Paris perfume; a small dark blue glass bottle held in a silver replica of the Eiffel Tower.

We were up early again on Easter Sunday, eagerly asking for our Easter egg. After much worrying Mam went into the pantry and reached up to the top shelf and brought out a paper bag which she handed to us. Inside were two Cadbury's cream eggs, one each, just like the little cream eggs you can buy today. We were quite happy with our little egg as we had never known any different, but one year I wandered outside and saw a girl who lived nearby with a huge chocolate egg. It was as big as a basin and marked on the surface like the grooves on a football. I had never seen anything like it before and ran in to Mam and gabbled out in amazement, 'Mam, you should see Helen Francis's Easter egg, it's huge!' I said. I described it to her in great detail.

'Well, said Mam, 'I don't know where her mother got that from, I'm sure.' And I believed her then.

DELIVERIES

Many more goods were delivered to the door when I was a child. Hardly anyone had a car. Except Mrs Hinks; she was the only one in the little community who owned a car, a smart, black saloon. She took the brides to church and expectant mums into the local cottage hospital when their time came, and fetched them home again with the new baby. Sometimes sailors knocked on her door if they wanted to be taken somewhere and there were no trains or buses. She didn't do it as a business, she was just a normal housewife, but she was always there when needed.

All the delivery men calling seemed to bring the community together. It brought women to their doors, or they collected in the street around the van, still wearing their pinnies and clutching their purses to their bosoms. It was one of their social occasions. They caught up with the gossip over the fence or called across the street to one another. 'Have you heard about Mrs Pegler, she's broken her ankle, fell down some steps she did last night.'

'Oh, dear, dear, dear,' exclaimed Mam, 'however will she manage.'

Or, 'Phyllis had her baby, a boy it was, seven and a half pounds' said another.

'Oh, how lovely!' cooed Mam.

I've mentioned Mr Sturge, the baker, and Mr Randall who sold fruit and vegetables from the boot of his car. We also had an ironmonger; a Mr Hillier called every two months in his big red van. I loved to accompany Mam out to watch him push up the sides of the van, like a roll-top desk, to reveal all manner of things. There were pots and pans, galvanised buckets shining silver in their newness all hooked up on high, crockery, cutlery, mops, tea strainers, brushes, pegs, anything and everything in the hardware line. And at the back of the van was a tap where Mr Hillier measured out paraffin into the waiting cans. I wandered around the van in awe and looked at all the goods; a shop on wheels. Mam made a few purchases; perhaps a couple of new basins for her Christmas puddings or an enamel pie dish.

The milk came in churns with a pony and trap from the nearby farm. The milkman measured out the milk with metal measures of a pint and half-pint straight into the housewives' jugs. The measures had hooks for handles and were hooked onto the top of the churn when not in use. The milkman had to knock on every door and wait for the owner, who then went off to find a jug, sometimes having to stop and wash one first, so it wasn't the quick plonking down of a couple of bottles on the doorstep. But, again, it was all about seeing people and stopping for a chat. Milk could only be bought from a dairy then. It seemed strange to me when we were able to go into a grocer's for a pint of milk.

The gasman came to empty the meter which was in the little cupboard under the stairs. Mam had fed it with pennies to enable her to have gas for the stove, and it had to be emptied regularly. Uncle Dave was our gasman. He was married to Dad's sister, Doris, and lived in the street. Working with gas left the smell in his clothes, and whenever you opened the door of his house the gassy smell hit you; it reeked of the stuff.

Uncle Dave was a lovely chap with red hair and a smiling, rosy face. Every Christmas he made an excuse to kiss Mam under the mistletoe; we never had any mistletoe but he still came. 'Oh, here's Dave coming for his Christmas kiss,' laughed Mam. And as I grew bigger he liked one from me too. He was a good musician and played the trombone in Sharpness Silver Band; he also played the mandolin and accordion.

When the gas manager retired Uncle Dave was made manager and moved into a lovely big house, not far from the street, but set on the edge of the canal with lovely views over the old dock. It was a square house with big rooms and lots of garden and I stayed there overnight sometimes with my cousin, Anita, for a treat. Our bedroom had its own walk in closet. The paper on the walls was topped with a border of bunches of grapes and I passed the time counting them while I waited for Anita to wake up in the mornings. And in the fireplace, to hide the empty grate, was a big photograph of the beautiful singer Alice Faye.

There was a huge gasometer not far away and there was also a chemical works surrounded by great piles of lime. Although we had been warned many times not to go near it because it would burn our skin, we could never resist standing before it and working our mouths to get a good mouthful of saliva and spit as hard as we could into the white stuff. We would watch in glee as it frothed and bubbled.

Uncle Dave emptied the meter and then sat at our scrubbed wooden table to count all the pennies. I sat and watched as he piled them high in columns; great piles of pennies all over our table. He talked to me and joked as he counted them. When they were all counted he gave some back to Mam to start her off again; a kind of rebate, as it depended how much gas she had used. The first pennies always clanked loudly as they fell into the empty meter.

The accumulator man was another caller who came regularly. The wireless needed a battery and it came in the form of an accumulator, a big, square, glass bottle full of acid. It had terminals on top to connect it to the back of the wireless with clips. 'The accumulator man is here!' shouted Mam, and Dad unhooked the old accumulator and exchanged it for the fully charged-one, which he connected to the wireless so that we were assured of being able to listen to music and the news again. The accumulator man came about once a fortnight and we paid him a shilling for the service.

After the war the fishmonger started to call again as well as the butcher. The fishmonger had a shop in Berkeley and brought fresh fish to Sharpness in his white van. No one had refrigerators, so meat or fish had to be used straight away.

We had a food safe; a small cupboard made of wood with panels of perforated zinc gauze in the sides and door to let in air but keep out flies. This was usually placed in the coolest part of the house. Meat delivered on a Saturday morning could go off by Sunday in the height of summer. Women had their own favourite way of trying to keep it fresh, such as wiping it with a cloth dipped in vinegar. Jugs of milk were stood in a bowl or bucket of water and covered with a tea-towel with the ends of the cloth just dipping into the water.

Frozen food was unknown, but I enjoyed seeing the Walls' 'Stop me and Buy One' man on a tricycle come into the street. He had a box on the side and from it sold water ices, lemon, strawberry or raspberry, and wafers, or he scooped up vanilla ice cream into our waiting bowls for our tea. What a treat!

Mr Williams came from the Co-op at Gloucester with vouchers, mutuality coupons Mam called them, and you could use them for anything you needed at the big Co-op store at Gloucester. They were in five shilling vouchers and you could have as many pounds' worth as you needed. Mr Williams then called weekly for the payment, which was marked on a card. When you had almost paid them off you could ask for some more.

Then there was Winnie Waldron. Mam got on well with her and always invited her in for a chat. I thought she looked like a man in her tweed suit, brogue shoes and with her dark, close cropped hair slicked back. She came from Hector Hayes, an outfitters in Berkeley, and brought with her a catalogue for Mam to look at and choose clothes from. She, too, came weekly for the money and passed on interesting bits of news while she did so. These methods were convenient for unexpected purchases, perhaps replacing something for the house or to pay for school uniforms.

Mam cycled to the Co-op at Newtown for her groceries. They gave out checks when you paid your bill; these were about as big as a bus ticket and Mam saved them up, storing them in all sorts of places such as the wooden biscuit barrel, which was never used for biscuits but for any odd bits and pieces, or in vases and pushed into drawers. When they were due to be counted, about twice a year, Mam frantically gathered them all up and tied them into bundles. We took them to the office above the Co-op store where they were counted, a very time-consuming operation, and then Mam received a rebate depending on how much she had spent at the Co-op. This extra money was always useful for sudden expenses, perhaps a new pair of shoes, a new kettle or a few luxuries at Christmas.

CHAPTER SIXTEEN

SCHOOLDAYS & AFTER

I was never an avid pupil. I went willingly enough, walking the mile there and back to the infants' class, where I traced my first letters or numbers in the tray of sand, or modelled in Plasticine, or if I was very good played with the doll's house. But after that, oh how I hated History and Geography; I found it so boring. And yet when I took it again years later as a mature student I loved every minute of it.

And Arithmetic. We had a Miss Stuart with steely grey set hair who was very strict. She never smiled but always picked on me to stand up and say my nine times table. I dreaded it. I got to eight times nine and began to falter, I looked around for some help from my classmates but there was none.

'Sit down,' she snapped, 'make sure you know it by tomorrow.'

I loved English, especially spelling tests. And I was one of the little group of children who were selected to go into the corner to practise joined-up writing. Pens with nibs were our writing tools. They were handed out each day and my pen always seemed to have a crossed nib. The inkwell always had balls of blotting paper shoved into it, and asking for a piece of blotting paper was like asking for gold.

For Physical Education we had to scrabble around in a box of plimsolls, or daps as we called them, and try to find a pair that fitted. That was a laugh. If I found one I could never find the other, and ended up with two left feet or two right, or one large and one so small that I could hardly cram my foot into it. But by then everyone was running outside and I had to manage, so off I went with my odd daps and did my games or exercises as best I could.

When we had music lessons I wasn't so pushy as some of the others, so I always ended up with the triangle, while the others had the tambourines or castanets.

Gaffer Watts, the headmaster, ruled with a rod of iron, or should I say the cane. He carried it with him everywhere. He used it, too; boys often had the cane for some misdemeanour, always on the palm of the hand, and they sported huge, raised, red weals afterwards. When we lined up after play to go back into school he stood by the window and rapped on it with his gold ring to beat the time for us to march in, 'one-two, one-two, one-two'. He took us for Music and just to make sure our mouths were the little round O he wanted when we were singing 'Nymphs and Shepherds' he came round and poked his cane between pupil's lips. Once he called out one of the girls and got her to stand on a chair with a pair of scissors and cut the hairs out of his ears. We were then in the last year of junior school. Can you believe it? I'm sure he relished it.

I shone at needlework. In the last year at junior school we were given a scrap of material and told to make something with it. Mine was a square of pink cotton, so I embroidered flowers in the corners and after hemming the edges I finished it off with blanket stitch all round and made it into a tray cloth. And it won a prize.

In my first year at grammar school we were asked to make something; it didn't have to be needlework, it could have been in wood or metal. I knitted a Fair Isle beret and mittens in pale yellow with green and brown. When the entries were judged, the head teacher called me out and asked me if my mother had assisted me. I pointed to the shaping of the crown of the beret and said she had shown me how to do the decreasing. Again I won a prize.

But there was a time when my needlework let me down. At the junior school we had been given a square of felt to work on during a sewing lesson. Mine was green and I had to embroider around the edge with blanket stitch. All was well until my thread got into a knot at the corner. I tried to sort it out, but the more I pulled the worse it became and felt being felt, with all my tugging it came away at the corner. A flap of felt was detached from the whole. I looked at it with shame. Worse still, one of the older bossy girls was on her way round checking pupils' work. She was just a few desks away and I willed the bell to go to save me; I watched with trepidation as she drew nearer.

She reached me and demanded to see my work. I said, 'No.'

'Right,' she said, 'I'm going to tell Miss Stuart.'

I slowly pulled it out from under my desk and offered it up.

'Oh!' she gasped when she saw it and marched to the teacher. I saw Miss Stuart's lips move. 'Whose work is this?' she demanded. The girl pointed me out and my insides squirmed as Miss Stuart glared at me. She cut out the knot and trimmed the corner and it was returned to me. The corner was no longer a right-angled one, but I carried on with my sewing, glad that it was over.

Anyway, in spite of all this I passed my Eleven-Plus exam and qualified to go to Dursley Grammar School. Mam was pleased and proudly fitted me out with a uniform and a strong leather satchel. I caught the school bus up on the High Road every morning after it had picked up children from Halmore, Purton and Hinton and we travelled the eight miles to Dursley.

My eyes were opened on going to Dursley Grammar School. The school, an extended house, was set in lovely grounds; there were shrubberies and huge fields for games and relaxing in at playtime. There were tennis courts, netball pitches and hockey fields. The library had a polished wood floor and the walls were lined with books from ceiling to floor. At Sharpness school we had had a box of books delivered occasionally, staying long after they had all been read.

The gymnasium was huge, with climbing bars around the walls and all necessary equipment. And I had my own daps. We always had assembly there each morning, when the masters and mistresses lined up on the stage in their flowing black cloaks.

There was a Science lab with Bunsen burners and pickled things in jars, and a Domestic Science room with all that was needed for cookery lessons and other forms of housewifery. We were taken out on trips too, perhaps to listen to a piano recital or climb Cam Peak as part of our Geography lesson. We went to the Regal cinema to see Laurence Olivier in Henry V, and a film of the complete Olympic Games which were held in London in 1948. No one had television sets then, so this was the only way to see the athletes perform. All this was new to me, as we had never left the school at Sharpness except to go on a march wearing our gasmasks, but there had been a war on after all.

Many subjects were new to me; French, English Literature, Algebra, Geometry, and games which included hockey, tennis and netball. But all this didn't mean I performed any better; I still had the ubiquitous 'must try harder' or 'could do better' on the bottom of my reports.

The teachers were strict. One, a Miss Sansum, was small in stature with glasses and dark hair scraped back in a bun: she took Geography and Religious Education. She was on dinner duty one day and always demanded silence. I was sitting with a friend on the bench at the dinner table and we both had our backs to her, so we didn't see her coming. My friend whispered something to me and I answered her and Miss Sansum crept up behind us and banged our heads together with an almighty crack. I saw stars!

Miss Sansum had a habit of day dreaming while taking a

lesson, and she would suddenly stop in mid-sentence and stare at the back of the class. Minutes would tick by and no one dared to move. After about ten minutes feet began to shuffle and books moved, and eventually she came to and carried on with the lesson. This often happened; perhaps it was to show she had full control.

By the time I was fifteen years old, the earliest age at which you could leave full-time education, my feet were itching. I had had enough of school and being shut up in the classroom; I wanted to be free and was glad to say goodbye to my schooldays.

And so I was out in the big world; but what to do? Mam wanted me to go into an office but I couldn't face that; it would be like school. I heard that an assistant was needed for a shop in Berkeley, so I cycled in to apply for the job.

Hector Hayes was a double-fronted shop with an outfitters on one side and a drapery and shoe shop on the other. Mr and Mrs Hayes lived at the back of the shop, where there was also a shoe repair workshop with three men employed and they were always kept busy.

My wages were to be £1/1/10d (£1.09p) weekly. Jean and Kath, the other assistants, were a little older than me. Jean was small and neat with dark brown curly hair and a pretty face. When her boyfriend, who was in the Navy, gave her his cast-off bell bottomed trousers of navy serge, she unpicked them and made an A-line skirt, the wide bottoms having enough fabric in each leg for the back and the front panels.

Kath had mid-brown curls and an open smiling face. She lived at Sharpness so we cycled in together, about three miles each way. It took us fifteen minutes, maybe slightly less on the homeward journey as we coasted down Station Hill, but we had to push our bikes up it in the morning. There was a bus if it rained, but we had to walk to Newtown for the bus stop and wait for it, so we were more independent on our bicycles. We cycled everywhere. Sometimes we cycled home for dinner then back again all in one hour. I was used to cycling to Berkeley, to the cinema or to see the doctor or dentist.

The outfitting side of the shop sold made-to-measure suits for men and women; also jodhpurs and hacking jackets. It was a good-class shop and there were plenty of well-off people in Berkeley. The honourable gentlemen brought in their dancing pumps to be repaired after dancing the night away at Cheltenham Town Hall to the music of Victor Sylvester and his orchestra.

I had an embarrassing moment when I had not been there long. Reps came from different firms to see Mr Hayes and we had to find out which firm they represented and then go and let him know there was one waiting to see him. One came into the outfitting department, and I asked which firm he was from. He gabbled out the name, so I asked him to repeat it and for all the world it sounded like 'Lop and Rabbit Company'. I knew that couldn't be right, but I was too embarrassed to ask again, so I went off to find Mr Hayes and told him a rep was in the shop for him.

'What company does he represent?' he inquired, to which I replied, 'I don't know.'

'Well,' he said, 'go and find out, Joyce.'

So back I went, thinking he must think I was really stupid, but I asked again and with a look of tired exasperation on his face he repeated it and it still sounded like 'Lop and Rabbit Co.'

I was in a fix. What should I do? Well, I just made myself scarce and disappeared up to the stockroom, which happened to be at the top of the building, hoping that one of the more experienced girls would sort it out. Which, of course, they did.

When I thought the coast would be clear and the rep gone I came down and peered into the shop and thank goodness it was empty. He was gone.

'Where have you been?' chorused the girls. 'Mr Hayes wants to see you immediately.'

So off I went, shaking in my shoes. I tapped on the door and went in. I should have told him that I didn't understand what the rep had said but I didn't. I had bluffed my way through it and he probably thought the worst of me. Anyway I was told off good and proper. 'And make sure you do the job properly next time,' he finished as I thankfully made for the door.

Well, the rep should have written it down, or better still, given me a card. How was I to know he was from the Dunlop Rubber Company.

I got on well with Jean and Kath. Every morning at 10.30 I went to the café across the road to get some rolls. They were freshly baked by Alpass' bakery just around the corner and were still warm and crispy from the oven. They were buttered and generously filled with grated cheese. I took these back and we made cocoa in the kitchen. Even now, a cup of cocoa and a cheese roll bring back happy memories.

Most of the time I served in the drapery side and every time new shoes came in they had me drooling. Mam had bought me plain black or brown lace-ups for school, or Clarks sandals for summer. Now all these fashionable shoes were within my grasp and I couldn't resist a few pairs.

'Go on Joyce,' urged Kath, 'take them on appro.'

'Yes,' said Jean, 'pay a bit off each week, it'll be all right.'

Soft navy blue kid trimmed with a button; red leather with a little bow and high heels, or beige strappy sandals. So I indulged myself.

After a year or two I was tired of shop work and wanted something different so I decided to leave. I had to tell Mam about the shoes, as I still owed some money on them. She was cross.

'What?' she yelled. 'They're not paid for. Just you go straight round to the Post Office my girl, and draw the money off your account and go and settle up. I won't have you owing money!'

So I did. It just wasn't done.

CHAPTER SEVENTEEN

DAIRYMAID

I was an outdoor girl and loved animals. My brother, Henry, worked on a farm, so I decided that I wanted to do the same, much to my mother's dismay. I heard of a farmer at Purton who needed someone for a milk round and to work in the dairy, so I cycled over to see about it. I found the farmer, Mr Phillips, hedging and ditching in a field bordering the road, and the interview was carried out over the hedge with me still straddling my bicycle.

It was arranged that I would start the following Monday. The journey was another three miles or more, along narrow country lanes and through villages; the roads were quiet, as there were very few cars then. I sometimes met the local bus or a farm tractor, but that was all.

My job was to do the milk round, which was with a pony and trap and took from 8am till about lunchtime. The milk was delivered in bottles then; I didn't have to worry about measuring it into jugs. After lunch I was to work in the dairy, washing and sterilising bottles. When the afternoon milking had begun I bottled the milk and put it in the refrigerator for the next day.

Purton is a lovely village on the River Severn; the canal runs through the middle of it, on its way to Gloucester. George, the present milkman, was to accompany me for the first few days and show me the ropes. He was a happy-go-lucky chap, middle-aged, short and stocky with skin the colour of mahogany thanks to the outdoor life he led. Brown eyes shone from a fleshy face and his head, although bald and shiny on top, sprouted tight red curls each side just to show you what might have been. He introduced me to the customers and showed me all the stopping places.

George always caught Darkie, the pony, and had him all harnessed up for me by the time I got there. Darkie was a sturdy little dark brown Dartmoor pony. On the way home George gave just one tap on his back with the reins and a gentle urging, 'Go-on Darkie, go-on,' and the pony's legs went like lightning: his hooves were lifted high into the air and each step came ringing down on tarmac. The crates of bottles rattled as we bowled along and we were soon home.

The round was five or six miles long, more if you count all the lanes where a few straggling houses were situated. And sometimes they were too narrow to take the pony and trap, so I carried the milk in crates and walked. After Purton was the hamlet of Hinton; a scattering of houses along the road, then on to Old Brookend and New Brookend, then Wanswell and Halmore and back to Purton. It was a circular route of narrow country roads bordered by fields, bluebell woods and wild daffodils. There were farm cottages in rows, and some larger houses of red brick and pretty thatched cottages with paths edged with flowers leading to a trellis porch. There were farms with their smells of silage, manure and pigs, barns full of sweet-smelling hay and yards littered with farm machinery.

The Cider House at Halmore used to be a drinking house but is now privately owned. We walked there from Sharpness on a Sunday afternoon when I was young and were allowed into the orchard, where we picked a big bunch of daffodils for sixpence to take home to our mothers. They were small, like the wild ones. Now I drove past it every day in the pony and cart.

On the corner of Halmore, just where the road veered left to lead back to Purton, there was a blacksmith. Many times I had ridden over from home with the pony to be shod. I would stand in the ramshackle shed and wait, gazing at all the old horseshoes hanging up and the tools of the trade. The blacksmith brought the fire to life with his bellows and when the flames roared up, the new shoes for the pony were held with a rod and pushed into them until they glowed red. He put the shoe over the anvil and great chimes rang out as he came down on it with his hammer, again and again. He lifted up the pony's hoof by grabbing at the hair on the fetlock and slapped the shoe on. It burned into it, sending up clouds of smoke and the smell of burning hoof. He blew away the smoke as he worked so that he could see what he was doing. When he was happy with the fit he tossed the shoe into a tank of water, where it sizzled and steamed until it was cool enough to be nailed on.

One bitterly cold day when I arrived, the blacksmith was nowhere to be seen. I hitched up the pony ready and waited for a while, but he didn't appear. The daughter of the house came to the door and called me inside. 'It's too cold for you to wait out there,' she said and told me to sit by the fire. It was a big old range with the oven on the side and the red hot coals glowed red behind the bars. I was glad to be warm.

The daughter got on with her ironing and after a while the blacksmith put his head round the door and said, 'Where's the young lady then?'. He smiled when he saw me sitting by the fire.

I soon got to know my customers on my milk round and they always welcomed me. At the very first house I called at in Purton, I was invited in for a cup of tea. It was a lovely red brick house with a large garden and the canal lying peacefully nearby. The tea was always scalding hot and liberally laced with demerara sugar; I couldn't hurry it, it was too hot, but it set me up for my morning of work and the Cooks, who lived there, liked to chat because I had been to school with their daughters and had stayed with them a few times.

There was just a main street at Purton with houses each side and a bridge over the canal with a few houses beyond. I knew many of the people, as some of the men worked at Sharpness, or I had been at school with some of the children and had stayed overnight with them.

I never had time for breakfast before I left home, so I called in at Ted Spill's shop when I reached it; it was the only shop there, and stood at the end of the main street through Purton. I was without restraint then and rationing was over, so I bought biscuits, usually ones with chocolate on both sides, or marshmallow teacakes. Ted weighed them out and tipped them into a paper bag and I nibbled them on my way round. At that time Lyons made individual fruit pies. They were in a square box and just right for a hungry one, with a variety of flavours – apple, apple and raspberry, apricot and blackcurrant. They were delicious.

I got to know all the customers and they treated me like a friend. 'Come on in and have a look at my new iron,' a voice called. 'Look, it runs on gas. See the little flame at the back?' I admired it. It ran on Calor gas and as she had neither gas or electricity in her little cottage it was a novelty and meant no more heating up irons on the fire.

Or I would hear, 'Come and see this jumper I've just finished for our Kath.' The owner of the voice led me across the garden to the hedge where a white, lacy jumper lay spreadeagled out to dry. Or Mrs White, who lived at the green wooden bungalow pleaded, 'Just come and have a look at this.' And inside a tiny kitten was curled up asleep in her slipper.

If anyone lived alone they specially enjoyed seeing me. They would pop out and look up the road to see if I was approaching, then dash back inside to put the kettle on. Miss Price was a spinster and always made a cup of tea for me. I admired her bright red geraniums lined up in the dark hall. 'I feed them with a drop of tea,' she said, 'they seem to like it.'

I made a lot of friends. 'Come on in and sit down,' said one, and waved me to a place in front of the Aga while she opened her cake tin and cut a slice of homemade fruit cake for me. Darkie knew all the stops and waited patiently. Sometimes he was rewarded with a sugar lump or a mint.

Ruby Turl lived at Halmore; a good-looking woman with a young family, she was well built with dark curly hair and dancing brown eyes. Halmore is off the beaten track. Just the bus goes through on its way to Gloucester, so with no shops and no transport of their own, people were stuck. They were poor people on farm labourers' wages, so they didn't go to town often.

Ruby wanted to knit a jumper for her daughter and asked me if I had any suitable patterns, as she knew I was a knitter. I looked some out and took a few for her to see. She chose one, but then she asked me to get the wool for her as well. 'I think green,' she mused, 'perhaps with an ounce of white.'

The wool shop was at Newtown, which meant a cycle ride of about a mile, and it was closed by the time I got home from work so I wasn't able to go straight away. Ruby used to look out for me and each day her eyes lit up when she saw me coming, but she soon looked downcast when I told her I hadn't been able to get the wool. She was so disappointed each time, so I knew I would have to make the effort. Eventually I cycled to the shop on my day off and chose some green wool for her – it was rather a vivid green but it was all there was – and an ounce of white. Wool, in those days, was sold in long skeins of one ounce each, and the shop owner was adept at holding all the wool you had bought with both hands outstretched, then twisting the skeins together until she had a tight coil. Then she pushed one end of the coil through the other and ended up with a fat twist of wool. It was then popped into a paper bag. At home the skeins had to be wound into balls and anyone willing would hold the skeins on their outstretched arms while the knitter wound it up.

The day I had the wool for Ruby her eyes lit up. She was so pleased that she couldn't wait to start knitting. It seemed that in no time at all she was holding up the finished jumper for me to see. The white yoke was studded with green flowers in a lazy daisy stitch and contrasted well with the bright green. Although I thought it was a bit of a bother at the time I was glad to have done something for her, especially when I read in the local paper of her death from cancer a few years after I had left the farm.

At another house in Purton I was invited to share their midday meal. Bill Mears worked on the dock at Sharpness and knew my family, so he insisted that I went every day and had a hot meal with them. My lunch hour was usually spent sitting on a bale of hay in the barn eating dry-as-dust sandwiches. I went nervously at first, afraid of intruding, but I was invited to sit at the table and Mrs Mears opened the oven at the side of the fire and pulled out my dinner. It was boiled bacon, potatoes and broad beans, hot and sizzling. From then on I always had my dinner with them. People were so kind.

One crisp winter morning I was walking along a bridle path. The grass was white and brittle under my feet and puddles were frozen over, showing bubbles of air moving under the ice. All was still and silent. A nearby collie dog stopped suddenly and sniffed the air. I stopped too, and then I caught the scent; the acrid smell of fox. I walked on cautiously and then I saw it. It was caught in a snare that had been placed over a hole in the hedge. It was a young fox, barely full grown, held tightly by its neck. It pulled away and thrashed and twisted as I approached and the noose tightened around its throat. I tied up the collie to keep it away, then went towards the fox again; I so much wanted to free it. I wore thick sheepskin gloves, so I put my hand towards it to try and loosen the wire, but it panicked and wouldn't let me touch it. I had another go and had my fingers nearly through the wire when the fox bit me. His sharp teeth punctured the leather with a pop and I felt the pain as it punctured my skin too.

I withdrew my hand and pulled off my glove and the blood trickled down my wrist. I looked at the fox sadly and knew I would have to leave it there. I untied the dog and carried on up the path where the farmhouse stood, and out in the orchard was the farmer calling to the hens as he threw the corn, 'Coop, coop, coop come on.'

'There's a fox down there,' I shouted, 'caught in the hedge.'

'No, can't be,' he called, 'I've checked this morning.'

'Well, there is,' I replied, 'about halfway down on the right.' I went on my way knowing he would go and finish the poor thing off.

The doctor laughed when I told him later how I got my

injury. 'You'd better come in and have a tetanus jab,' he said, 'they're pretty earthy creatures.'

Milk was delivered seven days a week, as hardly anyone had a fridge. I had to deliver on Christmas Day too, so I was careful not to take up too many offers of alcohol or I would not have been able to walk a straight line, even if Darkie could.

Wet weather was the bane of my life. I had to cycle to Purton to start with, a journey of three or four miles, and the milk float was open so I had no shelter at all. If I got up in the morning and heard the rain rattling on the corrugated roof of our lean-to, my heart sank. Another drenching, I thought. There was no man-made fabric as we know it today: no nylon, plastic or cosy quilted material. There were no anoraks, cagoules or parkas: just coats, short or long. Macintoshes were made of oilskin, gabardine or a rubberised fabric. The rubberised garments were expensive, so I sent for an oilskin I had seen advertised in the newspaper. When it arrived it was huge and black. I put it on and it was ramrod stiff and hung on me as unyielding as a tent. I pulled the belt in tightly round my tiny waist to try and control the excess fabric; at least it was waterproof, so I would just have to make the best of it. But after wearing it for a while the material began to crack and let in the rain. It was probably my fault for pulling in the belt and constantly creasing the oilskin. I often did the milk round absolutely soaked to the skin.

At Hinton there was a cottage where the Roberts lived, a pretty cottage with a trellis porch and a large garden full of flowers. It had once been part of a big estate and the Thorntons, who owned the estate, still lived in the grand, imposing manor, but the Roberts lived in a cottage built for the workers. I went to the grammar school with Jean Roberts, who lived there with her parents and younger brother. Jean was a year older than me, a pretty girl with brown eyes and dark curly hair; she was very popular with everyone. She came to the dancing classes with me and I always admired her. She was so alive and happy, always smiling. One evening, when she was about seventeen, she set off on the pillion of her boyfriend's motorbike. They were going to see a film at Gloucester, but at Cambridge, a notorious black spot, they were involved in an accident and were both killed. Helmets for motorcyclists were not compulsory then. They were buried together in the local churchyard at Berkeley. It was very sad. She was so lovely.

I delivered milk to the Roberts and had to walk past the front room window. My eyes were drawn to Jean's piano just inside and to the photograph of her on the top. She was smiling and looked just as I remembered her. I felt so sorry for the family.

One day the rain was pelting down and I was wet through once again. When I took the pint of milk to leave in the little trellis porch Mrs Roberts opened the door, which surprised me as I usually never saw anything of her. She was dumpy and motherly with brown eyes and grey curly hair.

'Would you like a raincoat?' she asked in a soft voice.

'Well, yes, I am pretty wet,' I stuttered. She disappeared inside while I waited in the porch, wondering what she would bring.

She came back with a light-coloured mac, the sort we used to call riding macs, and made of rubberised fabric, the kind I could never afford.

'It was Jean's,' she said quietly. 'You take it, it will help keep you dry.'

I smiled my thanks, and it did keep me dry. It was just my size and I loved wearing it. I was always grateful for her kindness in the midst of her loss.

I still think of Jean today and of a young life cut so tragically short.

My life on the farm and doing the milk round was not without its mishaps. At the end of the road through Purton, opposite Ted Spill's shop, was a turning to the right over a bridge which spanned the canal. A towpath ran alongside the canal and about two hundred yards or so along the towpath was a row of terraced cottages. It was a funny place to build houses, as their front doors opened straight out onto the towpath and the canal, and at the back was the vast expanse of the sandbanks of the River Severn.

I delivered milk to these cottages and I left Darkie on a patch of grass, where he usually grazed happily while I was away. On this particular morning I plodded along the path with a heavy crate of milk and delivered to each of the four houses; I didn't hang about as I never had any cups of tea from there. I was about halfway back along the towpath when I glanced up towards the bridge and was horrified to see the back half of the milk float hanging over the canal, with the crates of milk slowly disappearing into the murky water. A couple of chaps were holding Darkie's head and gently easing him away from the water. Several full crates of milk had disappeared into the canal and as the cart bumped on the grass I heard a few more slither in; they're probably still there. I had a full load on as I hadn't long left the farm.

All was well and one of the men went to the farm to tell them what had happened and to arrange for more milk to be brought to me while I went on with the round. Darkie was fine; he had got too near the water in his quest for fresh grass. But it was a good job the men were on hand.

The roads were very narrow. Sometimes the local bus would suddenly come round a bend, and I would have to get the pony and cart on the grass verge to give it room to get by. Just after leaving Purton on the way to Hinton is a hill; not terribly steep, but quite a pull for the pony with a full load of milk. But it was steep enough to cause me problems one morning in winter.

It was cold and frosty and there was ice on the road. All went well until we reached the hill. The float was heavy, and every time Darkie tried to get a grip his hooves slipped. I got down from the cart and held his head and soothed him as he was beginning to get a bit agitated. Then I tried to ease him forward, but each time his front feet slipped and he tossed his head and whinnied. He didn't like it one bit. I was scared of him going down and skinning his knees and maybe not being able to get up again with the weight of the cart on his shoulders.

It was a lonely road, and no one was likely to appear to help me. I stood for a moment wondering what to do, then I pulled Darkie on the grass verge and left him while I walked back to the nearest house. This happened to be Captain Duguid's fine house. I didn't deliver milk there so he didn't know me. The Captain was in charge of the *Vindicatrix*, the Sea Cadet Training School at Sharpness. I was worried at having to knock on the door of this rather imposing house, but there was nothing for it.

The Captain came to the door and I explained my problem in worried tones. 'I don't know what to do' I said, almost in tears.

He was very kind. 'Come in, come in my dear,' he said and took me to a room where there was a phone. He rang the farm, then handed the receiver to me so that I could tell Mr Phillips my trouble.

'Take some crates off Joyce,' he advised, 'leave them on the side of the road and I'll get someone to bring them to you in the van. Just take enough milk for the next village.'

So that's what I did. Most of the milk was left on the grass verge and then Darkie managed it up the hill without any more trouble. But I remember how scared and lonely I felt with no one about to help me.

Another mishap was rather more serious; Darkie bolted. Mr Phillips had four daughters between ten and four years of age and they liked to help me in the dairy. On this occasion I had just returned to the farm after finishing the milk round and Darkie was backed up to the dairy to enable me to unload the empty milk crates from the float and carry them into the dairy for washing and sterilising. When the float was empty, George always took Darkie away and released him from his shackles and let him run in the field until the next morning.

Two of the girls wanted to help me unload the cart, and as the crates were empty and light I let them have a go. I was in the dairy and I could hear them chatting and enjoying themselves. They must have tugged at a whole pile of crates and made them topple over, because there was an enormous crash as they fell over in the cart. The noise startled Darkie and he started off down the drive towards the road with such a lunge forward that the one girl was thrown clear. The other held on for dear life and screamed loudly.

Everyone on the farm was alerted by the noise and we all ran after the pony, but we were too late to stop him. He careered out of the gate, with just enough room at each side, turned right and galloped along the road with the girl still screaming loudly. We were all running along the road after him and I was thinking, 'Oh, my God, whatever is going to happen?' Luckily there was no traffic.

A couple of hundred yards along was a house on a bend in the road. The man who lived there was in his garden, and he had heard the noise. He ran out, waving his hands wildly in the air, and was just in time to halt the stampeding pony. Darkie stopped his mad gallop and by the time we arrived on the scene the man was holding his reins. I was so thankful. The girl was unhurt, but very frightened. The chaps walked back to the farm and Mr Phillips and I got into the cart to drive back.

Understandably Mr Phillips was angry and frightened for his

daughter's safety, so I got the sharp end of his tongue. 'And if it happens again I shall have to dispense with your services, Joyce,' he finished. I was so grateful to the man that stopped the runaway pony. He was brave and I hope Mr Phillips compensated him generously.

CHILDHOOD'S END

Being a seventeen-year-old female working with men had its drawbacks. They would sometimes get too close for comfort and push their faces close to mine, especially when I was in a situation such as holding two bottles under the bottler while the milk flowed in, when I couldn't push them away. But George was the most determined. He was married with several children, but that didn't stop him trying to get me in the straw. I didn't work closely with any of them but I saw them occasionally through the day, especially when I was waiting for the milk to come to the dairy in the afternoon. Sometimes I wandered to the milking shed to say hello to the cows and watch the pulsating machines drawing the milk from their fat udders.

There was an area, just before reaching the milking shed, where bales of hay and straw were stored for the cattle. On my return one day George crept up behind me and grabbed at me, demanding a kiss and trying to throw me down on the bales of straw. I squirmed to free myself from his grasp; he was so close I could see and smell the greasy sweat on his face. His eyes were wild. We grappled as he tried to hold me and force me down, but I wriggled free and hurried to the dairy where I felt safe in my own territory. I was careful after that, but it wouldn't have entered my head to complain to anyone about George's behaviour. It was just one of those things I accepted, one of the hazards of the job.

Living at 11 Bridge Road with my family and working on the farm was coming to an end. Someone special had come into my life and things were about to change forever. When I left the farm my customers showered me with presents; just small things for my future home such as a tray cloth, a couple of odd tablespoons or a china dish the colour and shape of a leaf.

At home on the 20th June 1953 the dark brown curtain was hauled back and the front door creaked open and I stepped out into the street as a young bride. A crowd of neighbours stood there waiting to see me in my finery and to wish me well as I climbed into the back of Mrs Hinks' car with Dad. I waved them goodbye as we set off for the church. Nothing would ever be the same again.

The boy often took a detour of the docks on his way home from school. He enjoyed seeing the ships that had come in and the cargo they were carrying. Now he stood on the quayside and gazed down into the hold of the ship. The dockers unloading the cargo smiled up at him; they were handling hessian sacks full of demerara sugar from Barbados. One had split open and the contents ran out like molten gold.

'Throw down yer cap then, Sunny Jim,' one man called, and the boy grabbed his hat and tossed it down to the men below. The man seized it and began to fill it with demerara sugar, scooping it up in handfuls. They passed it back up to the boy. He yelled his thanks and set off for home, holding his precious cargo close to his chest, leaping over coils of rope, heavy chains and railway lines as he ran.

'Mam, Mam look what I've got,' he called as he reached home.

'Well, I thought you would have found something cleaner to put it in,' his mother chided him. Nevertheless it was gratefully received and tipped into the glass sugar bowl to be enjoyed sprinkled on their porridge the next day.

That boy was later to be my husband, and when he told me this story I realized what an unusual childhood we had both had. We grew up in a busy port with ships coming from all over the world and had a freedom that is gone forever. Ships no longer come, swimming is not allowed in the canal and no one can catch elvers unless they have paid for an expensive licence or the River Patrol police will be out looking for them. The stacks of timber we played in are no longer there, and if they were, children would be kept well away.

The Severn Railway Bridge is now long gone. In October 1960 two tankers loaded with fuel oil, on their way to the docks from Swansea, ran into thick fog. They missed the dock entrance and as they were carried on up the river they became locked together. The vessels drifted on as far as the Severn Bridge and struck the pillars, demolishing two complete sections. The gas main on the bridge was fractured and sparks started a fire. The blazing oil set the river alight and five men lost their lives. By 1970 the bridge had been completely dismantled.

I loved listening to stories of times gone by. Whenever my husband and his brothers met up they talked of their grandfather who had run away to sea, having lied about his age. Born in 1868, Henry Clift was only nine when he was taken on by one ship to help the captain's wife, who had a young child. Wives usually accompanied their husbands on long voyages then.

One of his jobs was to wash the baby's nappies, and he told how he tied them all on to a rope so that they looked like the tail of a kite and fastened them to the stern of the vessel when it got underway. After a couple of hours he hauled them back on board ship, all lovely and clean, and hung them out to dry.

Whenever he docked at Bristol he walked home barefoot to Wanswell, near Sharpness, where he lived. What stories he could tell. I wanted to hear more. If only he had kept a journal.

I heard stories of how the crew of the steam tugs cooked their bacon and eggs for breakfast by putting them on the shovel and holding it over the roaring fire under the boiler. The steam tugs are gone too; the *Mayflower, Addie, Stanegarth, Iris, Resolute, Primrose* and *Speedwell*. Only the *Mayflower* remains, and she ferries sightseers around Bristol Docks.

From the High Road you could look down to the huddle

of houses with their smoking chimneys and long back gardens. About twenty years ago the 'powers that be' decided that the land where the houses were would be useful for a fertilizer factory, so they were demolished, but even today the ground is still empty.

I took my mother for one last look at the place where she had lived for over fifty years with my father. Our home looked like the houses I had seen in Bristol after the bombing of the war. The rooms were torn asunder, with wallpaper hanging in strips and the wood panelling of the landing and pretty Victorian fire grates of the bedrooms exposed to all.

Among the rubble my mother spotted a cushion. 'Oh!' she cried, 'my little cushion, I'll take that for my head.' But as she moved forward to pick it out a guard dog was upon us immediately, growling and snapping ferociously. 'Oh, save me, save me!' she whimpered, and as I moved forward to lead her back the guard of the site, in a caravan not far off, called the dog back. What had once been our home was now out of bounds.

Now, if I go back, the patch of land looks so small. I cannot believe that it supported a community for so many years. Some landmarks are still there, such as the Low and High Bridges and the archway at the bottom of the street that goes under a road where, during the war, we sheltered together from the bombs of Hitler. You try to get some idea of where the houses were where whole families lived out their lives. My father was born and died there; he never wanted to move away. I belonged there. Now they are gone, it is as if part of my life had gone too, vanished and lost. But it is still in my memory, so if I write it all down it won't be completely lost.

When I was young I spotted a yoke lying among other old farm memorabilia; the type used by milkmaids years ago to carry two pails of milk. I tried it on to see what it felt like on my shoulders and imagined a swinging pail of milk hanging on each side. I had mentioned this to my daughter, Diane, and recently we went, as a family, to the Farmer's Arms for a meal. As is the fashion now, old farm implements, pitchforks, rakes and shearing shears, decorated the walls. As we were being shown to our table Diane pointed to a yoke on the wall and said to my grandchildren, loudly so that everyone else could hear, 'Look, Nan used to wear one of those!'

Yes, it is definitely time to set the record straight.